fearless
dating

- ❤ ESCAPE the SINGLES WARD
- ❤ FIND TRUE LOVE
- ❤ and JOIN the HAPPILY MARRIED

fearless
dating

- ❤ ESCAPE the SINGLES WARD
- ❤ FIND TRUE LOVE
- ❤ and JOIN the HAPPILY MARRIED

Chris Deaver
Julia Deaver
Don McCartney

CFI
Springville, Utah

This is not an official publication of The Church of Jesus Christ of Latter-day Saints. The opinions and views expressed herein belong solely to the author and do not necessarily represent the opinions or views of Cedar Fort, Inc. Permission for the use of sources, graphics, and photos is also solely the responsibility of the author.

ISBN 13: 978-1-59955-341-2

Published by CFI, an imprint of Cedar Fort, Inc., 2373 W. 700 S., Springville, UT 84663
Distributed by Cedar Fort, Inc. www.cedarfort.com

LIBRARY OF CONGRESS CATALOGING-IN-PUBLICATION DATA

Deaver, Chris.
  Fearless dating : escape the singles' ward, find true love, and join the
happily married / Chris and Julia Deaver and Don McCartney.
    p. cm.
  ISBN 978-1-59955-341-2
  1. Dating (Social customs)--Religious aspects--Church of Jesus Christ of
Latter-day Saints. 2. Courtship--Religious aspects--Church of Jesus Christ
of Latter-day Saints. I. Deaver, Julia. II. McCartney, Don, 1978- III.
Title.

  HQ801.D436 2009
  248.8'4--dc22
                        2009032738

Cover design by Angela D. Olsen
Cover design © 2009 by Lyle Mortimer
Edited and typeset by Megan E. Welton
Printed in the United States of America

10 9 8 7 6 5 4 3 2 1

Printed on acid-free paper

Dedication

We dedicate this book to our parents Tom and Devi Deaver, Vernon and Penelope Gantt, and Ed and Cynthia McCartney—who have given us great examples of how to make an eternal marriage work (and fun) every day.

Chris—I dedicate this book to Julia
for being my true companion.

Julia—I dedicate this book to Chris
for showing me what dreams are made of.

Don—I dedicate this book to The Original Knights,
and to the countless young women that I've dated.

Contents

Foreword

When I was quarterbacking in the NFL, I often had to throw the ball over huge defenders without knowing exactly where it would land. My coach told me that this was something that required a leap of faith. By believing that the receiver would be there as I threw the ball, I was able to connect for touchdowns. Similarly, dating effectively in a Christ-centered way takes a leap of faith, as well as following great coaching from Heavenly Father. You may not know how everything will turn out in the end, but by staying focused and listening to the Spirit, you will ultimately achieve success.

I remember being single and what it was like to go through the experience of dating. I also recall feeling the desire to make the best decisions. One thing that I have learned is that going from single to happily married for time and all eternity takes effort and energy. Most of all, it takes selflessness.

Dating is filled with decisions. And making the best decisions means being your best self and moving forward with faith. This book will help you do that. It's a great playbook for true dating success. Loaded with advice from the scriptures and great examples, *Fearless Dating* can make a difference for any single Latter-day Saint looking to confidently prepare for a great marriage.

—Steve Young, Quarterback and Pro Football Hall of Famer

A Note from the Authors

Latter-day Saint singles everywhere are dating, trying to find that special someone to marry for time and all eternity. Some have recently started down that path and have no idea where to begin. Others are still searching, and some are *totally* frustrated. And yet, dating will always be the path toward eternal marriage and everlasting joy.

As we interviewed hundreds of single and married people and read countless articles on the subject of dating, we discovered one key that makes the difference in achieving results. It isn't some homespun remedy that guarantees instant dating success. Instead, it is a powerful yet simple principle that makes dating for a great marriage not only possible but also full of opportunity. It is confidence. Paul declared, "Cast not away therefore your confidence, which hath great recompence of reward" (Hebrews 10:35).

We invite you to become a confident, fearless dater. To do so is to embark on a great adventure and pursue your own promised land with optimism, knowing that success doesn't happen in a single day. The Lord will guide you as you walk with Him in this all-important chapter of your life.

This book is not for the passive observer. Fearless dating is not a spectator sport. It requires serious effort. This book is designed to be studied one chapter per week, so that you fulfill each commitment before moving on to the next chapter. In each new chapter you will be given a new dating commitment. Fulfill each dating commitment, no matter how awkward it may seem at the time, and you will experience powerful results. And, as a result, *you* will become a fearless dater!

As you engage in fearless dating, get connected and share your stories at www.fearlessdatingbook.com; on *Fearless Dating*'s fan page on facebook; or on twitter @fearlessdating. The best stories will be entered into a drawing to win an all-expense paid Dream Date!

—Chris, Julia, and Don

Part 1:

Be Your Best Self

1

Plan for Success

Opening Your Eye of Faith

Have faith to seek first the kingdom of God. We have learned that unshakable faith in the Lord enriches married life and love. Faith in Him increases one's very capacity to love, both quantitatively and qualitatively.—Elder Russell M. Nelson[1]

Maybe you've been home from a full-time mission for a only month or two and have recently happened upon the serious dating scene. Maybe you're just arriving at that stage in life when you feel comfortable with focusing on dating as a real priority. Whatever your situation, you can surely relate to the feelings of so many singles we know and love. Yes, they want to have fun. And yes, they eventually want to get married. Some are doing everything they can to find the right person with whom they can settle for time and all eternity. Some may even be so anxious to have their dream wedding that they feel like they may have forgotten the real goal. In reality, there is a plan of salvation and exaltation for you, and dating has everything to do with it.

Preparing for success in dating is like making a great movie. It all starts with envisioning a great story. If the writer and director don't believe they can make a great story, the whole thing will fail. Imagine the actors standing around on set, waiting to deliver lines and perform actions that ultimately lead them nowhere—no final destiny, no game-winning touchdown, no buried treasure, no fair maiden, and no crystal shores. It is an unfortunate end to what could have been a great "happily ever after" and yet, far too often, it's exactly what happens to those who date without an ultimate goal in mind.

Plan for success in dating by writing your story. It doesn't necessarily have to be written in pen and ink, but your success story needs to be created, stored in your mind, and recalled daily. It needs to be something you not only believe in, but something you have imagined and are prepared to pursue at all costs, always following the Savior's oft-repeated counsel to "be of good cheer."[2]

Envision in your mind a beautiful scene where your wonderful spouse awaits, prepared to embrace you for who you are. Ponder what it feels like to love and be loved deeply; to care and be cared for; to serve and be served. What is it like to exchange meaningful feelings and thoughts with someone with whom you will spend the rest of eternity, someone with whom you will share your heart? Consider the joy you will experience as you begin to better see and understand the love of the Savior and the eternal joy that He has promised.

In this world, you are searching for eternal treasure. It will certainly take great effort to discover, but fortunately, the Lord has provided the treasure map through his prophets. President Thomas S. Monson has said, "I wish to provide the three pieces of your treasure map to guide you to your eternal happiness. They are: (1) learn from the past, (2) prepare for the future, (3) live in the present."[3]

It should not be a surprise to anyone that we learn from the past but that we live in the present. How does this apply to dating? If you are constantly reminiscing and reliving your past dating relationships in your mind, you will miss the opportunities of the present.

 All that you achieve and all that you fail to achieve is the direct result of your own thoughts.—James Allen

The restored plan of happiness provides all the answers you need to make dating a success in your life. In the scriptures, the Lord tells us to see with "an eye of faith" (Alma 32:40). And although that may be fairly easy to do in such things as missionary work and priesthood blessings, is it any surprise that He expects it in dating? But how exactly are we supposed to see with "an eye of faith" in dating? First, we must understand what dating is and what it is not. As with anything of eternal consequence, we must view dating as an activity that is both temporal and spiritual.

Set your sights on this great adventure of love and marriage. Plan for dating success. Know that as you do His will, Heavenly Father—the Governor of the Universe and everything in it, as well as the literal Father of your Spirit—is bound to bless you (see D&C 82:10). Remember also that it will be on the Lord's timetable that these blessings come. So, if you are well over twenty-five and starting to feel the pressure to get married, or you are just back from your full-time mission and barely beginning your search, or you are exhausted by the dating scene altogether, then it's time to focus on being a part of your adventure in dating.

Be Led by the Spirit

Let's face it: finding the right companion is a challenge. Sometimes the search can seem like a daunting task. For those who have encountered the frustrations of rejection, heartbreak, and shattered hopes, it may even seem impossible. Fortunately, in this life, you are not alone. You have been blessed with parents, teachers, and friends who are truly concerned for you. Most important, when you were confirmed a member of the Church of Jesus Christ of Latter-day Saints, you were given an unequaled blessing that provides comfort, peace, and pure knowledge—the gift of the Holy Ghost.

In our lifetime, we may not be asked by the Lord to retrieve plates of brass or kill the wicked thugs who possess them. But, like Nephi, we have the goal to get to our own "promised land" of a happy marriage and family. And, like Nephi, we practice obedience and are "led by the Spirit" to pursue these blessings.

Through obedience to the promptings of the Holy Ghost, you are given knowledge of "all things what ye should do" (2 Nephi 32:3). This promised power can be realized in dating. This doesn't mean that the Lord will do the work for you. The Lord declared, "Verily I say, men should be anxiously engaged in a good cause, and do many things of their own free will, and bring to pass much righteousness" (D&C 58:27).

Spiritual promptings in dating come through hard work and effort, often amid rejection, feelings of inadequacy, and even pride. But the Lord will lead you by the Spirit if you are willing to be led. When you are led by the Spirit, you have no interest in dating someone with low standards. You are focused on the cause of righteousness and concerned with the eternal results your actions will bring. You regard this cause as the greatest priority because it will lead to so many other blessed opportunities in this life and the next.

Jessica S., one of the single women we interviewed says, "Following your gut feeling, or the Spirit, is so important in dating. It really means everything."

Marrying the right person in the right place at the right time is a miracle. If it is to be eternal, it will not come easily. Exaltation is not a cheap experience. If you exercise great effort and energy in this quest, you will find powers beyond your own through the Spirit.

Find Success through the Atonement

As a member of the Quorum of the Twelve, President Henry B. Eyring offered this counsel to members of the Church: "It is hard to know when we have done enough for the Atonement to change our natures and so qualify us for eternal life. And we don't know how many days we will have to give service necessary for that mighty change to come. But we know that we will have days enough if only we don't waste them."[4]

Seeking your spouse in the right way requires strength found only in the Atonement of Jesus Christ. The best kind of dating, the kind that leads to exaltation, takes your best efforts. This concept may seem foreign to some people, but it is nevertheless true. Jesus Christ said it himself when he uttered the powerful words, "I am the way, the truth, and the life" (John 14:6). He didn't add any caveat or condition like "only when you are married and have a family." No, Jesus Christ will provide the path for you at every stage of your life. Dating may seem like an unconventional or totally new path for you—but it will certainly be right. And just as Jesus Christ literally stands at the head of His Church, He will stand at the head of your dating efforts if you allow Him to, and He will lead you in the right path.

If you have ever put your heart on the line, you know that dating often involves struggling through challenges. This phase of life, more than any other before it, is a time for the Savior. It is a time for seeking the Great Healer, who can restore and strengthen anything He touches. It is a time to rely on the power of the One who knows and understands everything in the universe, including your dating life.

Many years ago, in a land far away, the great prophet Isaiah declared,

"But they that wait upon the Lord shall renew their strength; they shall mount up with wings as eagles; they shall run, and not be weary; and they shall walk, and not faint" (Isaiah 40:31).

So it is with each of us. As you take the Lord at His word, believing with all your heart that he will empower you, you will be given all the strength you need. Many people who are happily married now remember vividly the struggles and challenges they had when they were single and searching for that special someone. Those who dated fearlessly tell brightly of the joys they experienced alongside the challenges they faced, and of coming to know the Savior so much more during that special time of their lives. Sister Kathleen H. Hughes said:

> The Savior's invitation is clear and direct, and importantly for us, it is constant: 'Come unto me, all ye that labour and are heavy laden. . . . Take my yoke upon you, . . . for . . . my burden is light' (Matthew 11:28–30). This is the Lord's promise to me and to you.
>
> My prayer for each of us is that we will remember when the Lord has spoken His peace to us and has encircled us in the arms of His love. And just as important, will you, if you haven't felt that love for a while, seek to see it and feel it as you go about the ordinary tasks of your life. As you do this, over the days and months and years of your life, the memories of those interactions with the Lord will become sweet gifts to open a second time—or many times—to bolster you when life is difficult.[4]

Because of the Atonement of Jesus Christ, we feel His love. When we apply the Atonement in our lives, we receive powerful knowledge of how we should act in any given situation. The Savior has empowered you to become like Him. This potential is certainly intimidating to anyone who has tried to emulate Jesus Christ—even for a day—only to fail in countless ways. Yes, we are imperfect and yes, we will fail before we succeed. But the perfection of our souls is available and alive in our emulation of Jesus Christ. In the book *Mere Christianity*, Lewis offers this memorable guidance:

> May I start by putting two pictures, or two stories rather, into your minds? One is the story you have all read called Beauty and the Beast. The girl, you remember, had to marry a monster for some reason. And she did. She kissed it as if it were a man. And then, much to her relief, it really turned into a man and all went well. The

other story is about someone who had to wear a mask; a mask that made him look much nicer than he really was. He had to wear it for years. And when he took it off he found his own face had grown to fit it. He was now really beautiful. What had begun as a disguise had become a reality.[5]

Emulating the Savior is the best way to truly worship Him. As we grow to become like Him, little by little, we pave the way for the truest type of success we can achieve: preparing for eternal life through a temple marriage. At the end of the day, how close or how far we come to eternal life is all that really matters. Thankfully, the Atonement of Jesus Christ is grand enough and great enough to cover all our sins, to reach every challenge we have, and to bring us peace in the very moment it is needed. This peace comes as we center our lives on the Savior. Just as He is central to the plan of our Heavenly Father, the Savior must be central to our individual lives for us to experience true happiness.

Pray with Power

Throughout the scriptures, the Lord has repeated His counsel for us to pray. Not only does He expect us to pray, but He also expects us to do so with sincerity, hope, and intensity of feeling. Have you ever wept while praying to the Lord? When was the last time you truly felt the Lord had answered your prayers? The Lord clearly stated His expectation and promise for us when He said, "Therefore, if you will ask of me you shall receive; if you will knock it shall be opened unto you" (D&C 6:5).

Tom was single and had dated for many years to find his eternal companion. He was sad and tired because things had not worked out as he had hoped. He was frustrated with his failure. His feelings of sadness continued until one day, he found himself in his apartment, feeling extremely alone. Sitting at his desk and feeling the cold, dark reality of his situation all about him, Tom started to cry. As he cried, he lifted his voice to the Lord and explained his feelings and desires to meet a wonderful woman with whom he could fall deeply in love and whom he could serve for the rest of his life. Soon, Tom felt the love of the Savior fill his heart and the courage to press on in his endeavor to the find the woman he would marry.

We can see the plan of happiness unfold in our lives through our discipleship. When we allow our will to be swallowed up by the will of God, fearing no loss of popularity or personal comforts, and are willing to exchange everything, even our "kingdom" (see Alma 22:15), and can let go of our selfish feelings and thoughts, we will be filled. In essence, becoming humble is a necessary prerequisite to true power, just as an Olympic runner must kneel, wait, and listen for the signal before bursting forward in an explosion of energy. We look up to that Supreme Being whose form is not mystical or impossible to imagine. Heavenly Father is totally committed to our growth, progress, and fulfillment. Beyond this, Heavenly Father possesses all the resources to achieve every objective, with a perfect knowledge, omniscience, justice, mercy, and divine love. His is a fatherly concern, grown of literal roots. For He is our true Heavenly Father, and He has watched us and known each of us from the beginning.

More than anything else, prayer strengthens you to *become* the right person so you can *find* the right person. Prayer prompts you to do the things necessary to qualify for the great blessing of marrying that special spouse so you can raise a righteous family together. In his intercessory prayer, Jesus asked that the Apostles might be one with Him, as He is with the Father (see John 17:20–23). In your prayers, ask that you may be one with the Lord and that you may prepare yourself to be one with that special someone you seek. Trust in the Lord.

Regarding prayer and dating, Jane A. states, "I always pray before a date. I pray for my date and for me, and I pray that we have a good time and that we come away having learned something. Afterwards, it has been obvious for me whether or not to go out with someone again. Always pray before a date."

President Gordon B. Hinckley said that you should "kneel alone in prayer before [you] leave home on a date that [you] may remain in control of [yourself], that [you] will so conduct [yourself] that the evening will provide a beautiful and wonderful experience and not something that can only bring later regret."[6]

The Lord declares, "Wherefore, ye must press forward with a steadfastness in Christ, having a perfect brightness of hope, and a love of God and of all men. Wherefore, if ye shall press forward, feasting upon the word of Christ, and endure to the end, behold, thus saith the Father: Ye shall have eternal life" (2 Nephi 31:20).

Prayer is powerful in helping you keep perspective on the true Giver of gifts. When many of his contemporaries sought the praises of the world for their great discoveries and achievements, Christopher Columbus emphasized regularly that he was led by God to achieve the glory of God. This was evidenced in Columbus's first act in the New World: he fell to his knees in humble prayer. Prayer is the starting point for success in achieving your worthy dreams. It will empower you as you make your efforts sincere, heartfelt, and direct. Speak to Heavenly Father with all your heart, and listen closely to His direction. This means that while you pray, it's important to listen quietly and pay attention to the feelings that the Lord places in your heart.

The Lord answers prayers, and how He does so is something very important for you alone to discover as you pray about dating and whom you should marry. Elder Richard G. Scott shares the following:

> Often when we pray for help with a significant matter, Heavenly Father will give us gentle promptings that require us to think, exercise faith, work, at times struggle, then act. It is a step-by-step process that enables us to discern inspired answers. . . . Seldom will you receive a complete response all at once. It will come a piece at a time, in packets, so that you will grow in capacity. As each piece is followed in faith, you will be led to other portions until you have the whole answer. That pattern requires you to exercise faith in our Father's capacity to respond. While sometimes it's very hard, it results in significant personal growth.[7]

Sometimes people think it is trivial to pray about certain day-to-day things like dating. They may think that Heavenly Father is only interested in major things like parting the Red Sea, moving mountains, and building temples. The reality is that nothing could be further from the truth. Heavenly Father is just as interested in you and your particular problems and challenges as He is in anything else He does in the world. In fact, you are His greatest work (see Moses 1:39). The scriptures are filled with words of encouragement to counsel with the Lord in all things.

> Therefore may God grant unto you, my brethren, that ye may begin to exercise your faith unto repentance, that ye begin to call upon his holy name, that he would have mercy upon you;
> Yea, cry unto him for mercy; for he is mighty to save.

Yea, humble yourselves, and continue in prayer unto him.

Cry unto him when ye are in your fields, yea, over all your flocks.

Cry unto him in your houses, yea, over all your household, both morning, mid-day, and evening.

Yea, cry unto him against the power of your enemies.

Yea, cry unto him against the devil, who is an enemy to all righteousness.

Cry unto him over the crops of your fields, that ye may prosper in them.

Cry over the flocks of your fields, that they may increase.

But this is not all; ye must pour out your souls in your closets, and your secret places, and in your wilderness.

Yea, and when you do not cry unto the Lord, let your hearts be full, drawn out in prayer unto him continually for your welfare, and also for the welfare of those who are around you.

And now behold, my beloved brethren, I say unto you, do not suppose that this is all; for after ye have done all these things, if ye turn away the needy, and the naked, and visit not the sick and afflicted, and impart of your substance, if ye have, to those who stand in need—I say unto you, if ye do not any of these things, behold, your prayer is vain, and availeth you nothing, and ye are as hypocrites who do deny the faith. (Alma 34:18–28)

· ·

1. Russell M. Nelson, "Faith and Families," *Ensign*, Mar. 2007, 36–41.

2. See Matthew 14:27; Mark 6:50; and John 16:33 for just a few instances of this commandment.

3. Thomas S. Monson, "Treasure of Eternal Value," *Ensign*, Apr. 2008, 4–9.

4. Kathleen H. Hughes, "Remembering the Lord's Love," *Ensign*, Nov. 2006, 112.

5. Henry B. Eyring, "This Day," *Ensign*, May 2007, 90.

6. Gordon B. Hinckley, "A Challenging time—A Wonderful Time, An Evening With President Gordon B. Hinckley," Address to CES Faculty, February 7, 2003.

7. Richard G. Scott, "Using the Supernal Gift of Prayer," *Ensign*, May 2007, 9.

Week One Commitment: Plan with an eye of faith by praying sincerely to Heavenly Father for direction in your dating efforts. Set the goal of praying daily all this week for help in dating. Listen closely to the promptings of the Spirit. Write them down and act on them. And remember, the Lord is there for you.

Notes

2

Be Confident

Letting Your Best Self Shine

While here, we have learning to gain, work to do, service to give. We are here with a marvelous inheritance, a divine endowment. How different this world would be if every person realized that all of his actions have eternal consequences. How much more satisfying our years may be if in our accumulation of knowledge, in our relationships with others, in our business affairs, in our courtship and marriage, and in our family rearing, we recognize that we form each day the stuff of which eternity is made. . . . Life is forever. Live each day as if you were going to live eternally, for you surely shall.—President Gordon B. Hinckley[1]

So, you are praying in earnest about dating, and have thus begun the journey of dating for a great marriage. This is wonderful! Keep it up, and you'll be blessed tremendously. Fearless dating, however, requires even more than powerful prayer.

Too many Latter-day Saint singles feel deflated, weak-kneed, or even flustered when it comes to dating. If you meet someone who doesn't look like they feel this way, they probably just aren't showing it. The only prescribed cure for this problem is true confidence. But if confidence is the key to successful dating, how do you develop it? We hope you will answer this question for yourself by the end of this chapter.

 If I have lost confidence in myself, I have the universe against me.—Ralph Waldo Emerson

Confidence is necessary for effective dating. Real confidence comes through righteous living, exercising faith, and repentance. In the scriptures, confidence is also called hope. By doing the right things daily, you increase hope in your life. Hope and doubt cannot coexist. Expressing this principle in more powerful words, the Lord lovingly challenged us, "Look unto me in every thought; doubt not, fear not" (D&C 6:36).

Be Your *Best* Self

Hope is more than just positive thinking. Often people give the advice to "just be yourself," as if it were the solution to any problem. If just being yourself were the answer to discovering true happiness, then every person on earth who was "just being themselves" would be experiencing sublime joy despite trials and challenges. This just isn't the case. The only time "success" comes before "work" is in the dictionary. The only path to dating success is found in being your *best* self, whatever that means for you, and however the Lord defines that for your life.

Imagine the scene: along a highway, you see a green dot, far off in the distance. It seems to be getting closer to you, but you're not sure. Then, a white burst of light flashes past you. You turn your head just in time to recognize the fluffy white tail of a rabbit hopping over the hill ahead, zipping zealously along at incredible speeds. As you inspect the highway, you realize it's actually a track, and the bunny is outpacing the green dot in the distance by a ridiculously advanced rate. *Whatever that green thing was*, you think to yourself, *it's never going to see the backside of that rabbit again.* Then, you lie down in the grass next to the road for a quick nap.

As your eyes close, you feel transported by the warm yellow light of day. Suddenly you hear a "clump, clump." Again, "clump, clump." Only, it's getting louder every minute. You open your eyes to see that the green dot in the distance was not a wandering watermelon or a bouncing bush, but a turtle! And this turtle is plodding along right past you, as if trying to catch that rabbit. It is by far the funniest thing you have ever seen. The turtle is so slow you could literally run several circles around it while it crawls, but out of respect for the little critter, you choose not to. Instead, you follow slowly. As the turtle comes up the hill, you're sympathetic. This race is already done, you think. That rabbit must have won an hour ago. But, to your utter surprise, you see the rabbit sitting off to the side of the road, under a tree, talking on his cell phone. And as the turtle ever so slowly moves by the rabbit and past the finish line, you almost want to shout out at the rabbit, to alert him that he's about to lose the race. But the rabbit looks so enthralled in his conversation that you decide not to bother him.

You have undoubtedly heard of "The Tortoise and the Hare" before, or, as we like to call it, "The Little Turtle Who Could." However, you probably haven't heard how it relates to dating and marriage. When it comes to dating and marriage, most of us relate better to the turtle than the rabbit. After all, the rabbit didn't win. In fact, he lost to one of the slowest animals on the planet! At the end of the day, it was because the rabbit was "just being himself"—quick to start but not focused on enduring. The turtle, however, kept his eye on the finish line and ran as quickly as his stubby legs would allow. He progressed little by little, moving forward one step at a time, being his best self.

The turtle had every reason in the world to believe that he could not possibly win the race. Yet, in spite of the odds, the turtle was very confident that he could win the race. He knew that by putting himself in the right place at the right time, and by taking the right steps, he would win in the end. He didn't waste his time hopelessly comparing himself to the rabbit—he just took initiative and made things happen. Like the turtle, you must be your best. Don't compare yourself to anyone but you.

 I always had the ultimate goal of being the best, but I approached everything step by step.
—Michael Jordan

John D. says, "For a long time I felt like I wasn't a catch. But I later realized that someone who is not confident is automatically not much of a catch. Without becoming arrogant, it is important to be positive about the good attributes that you have to offer. Do what you can about the things that you view as your shortcomings and recognize that you don't have to be perfect. Be your best and great things are bound to happen."

Confidence is a focus and a feeling that comes over time, and must not be forgotten in an instant. When the worries of the world press down on you, as they certainly will, it can be tempting to forget how the Lord always stands ready to support you. Elder Jeffrey R. Holland expressed:

13

I would like to have a dollar for every person in a courtship who knew he or she had felt the guidance of the Lord in that relationship, had prayed about the experience enough to know it was the will of the Lord, knew they loved each other and enjoyed each other's company, and saw a lifetime of wonderful compatibility ahead—only to panic, to get a brain cramp, to have total catatonic fear sweep over them. They "draw back," as Paul said, if not into perdition at least into marital paralysis.

I am not saying you shouldn't be very careful about something as significant and serious as marriage. And I certainly am not saying that a young man can get a revelation that he is to marry a certain person without that young woman getting the same confirmation. I have seen a lot of those one-way revelations in young people's lives. Yes, there are cautions and considerations to make, but once there has been genuine illumination, beware the temptation to retreat from a good thing. If it was right when you prayed about it and trusted it and lived for it, it is right now. Don't give up when the pressure mounts. You can find an apartment. You can win over your mother-in-law. You can sell your harmonica and therein fund one more meal. It's been done before. Don't give in. Certainly don't give in to that being who is bent on the destruction of your happiness. He wants everyone to be miserable like unto himself. Face your doubts. Master your fears. "Cast not away therefore your confidence." Stay the course and see the beauty of life unfold for you.[2]

Your dating and marriage story is going to be different than anyone else's. Don't worry. If you start this journey by working on yourself, focusing on each day and each moment as it happens, you will eventually cross that finish line of exaltation having done your best.

Dane W. says, "I have to be the best that I can be. If someone doesn't like that and if someone thinks I'm fat or too tall or whatever that's fine. I'm being the best that I can be. And I will meet, date, and marry the woman for me who is being the best that she can be and to whom I'm attracted."

Christian T. adds, "Dating helps you find out more about who you are and who you want to be. Anytime that you want to be your best is a time you can receive inspiration and be motivated to improve."

Build, Build, Build

Elder Joseph B. Wirthlin taught, "I urge you to examine your life.

Determine where you are and what you need to do to be the kind of person you want to be. Create inspiring, noble, and righteous goals that fire your imagination and create excitement in your heart. And then keep your eye on them. Work consistently towards achieving them."[3]

Darrel M. says, "Don't compare yourself with other people, because the bottom line is that everybody's different. We are all sons and daughters of God with unique, divine potential."

Confidence, like a majestic building, is built one piece at a time. Think of what it took to construct the Salt Lake Temple—literally forty years of hard labor! Your success in dating will not likely take that long (and if it does, bless your soul), but it will definitely take constancy, hard work, and effort. Even after you're married, you will need to continue to work hard. You and your spouse will be doing something totally new, something you've never—not even in the pre-mortal life—done before! So, start building now, and never stop. Along the way, it is important to remember that building yourself is not an issue of comparing yourself to anyone else.

General young men and young women leaders have offered this advice: "You might ask: 'How can I do this? Is there something to guide me?' Yes, there is. The principles and doctrines in *For the Strength of Youth* will guide you to make decisions that will qualify you for the companionship of the Holy Ghost. And if you have the Holy Ghost with you, you are, in a sense, living in the presence of God. Think of the confidence Heavenly Father has in you to send you His Spirit."[4]

As you qualify for the companionship of the Holy Ghost, you naturally improve your life. This means more, not less pondering on who you need to become. Elder Neal A. Maxwell of the Quorum of the Twelve offered this counsel: "If the choice is between reforming other Church members [your date, fiancé, spouse, or children] or ourselves, is there really any question about where we should begin? The key is to have our eyes wide open to our own faults and partially closed to the faults of others—not the other way around! The imperfections of others never release us from the need to work on our own shortcomings."[5]

Start improving yourself by taking an honest inventory of who you are and who you want to be. Take the time to do this at least once a week. Spend thirty minutes to an hour each week thinking about who you are, what you have achieved, and what your mission in this life is. Remember to *balance* your focus on building your strengths and fixing weaknesses. Some people make the mistake of thinking only about what they lack, and that can be depressing.

The Lord promises, "If ye are prepared ye shall not fear" (D&C 38:30). This is totally applicable to dating. Prepare yourself by building on your existing foundation, no matter what state it may be in. Prepare yourself for situations by ensuring you are totally committed to who you are and who you want to be in life. As you build yourself with the focus on discovering your strengths, you will definitely notice weaknesses. Remember, this is the Lord's prescribed way of doing things: "And if men come unto me I will show unto them their weakness. I give unto men weakness that they may be humble; and my grace is sufficient for all men that humble themselves before me; for if they humble themselves before me, and have faith in me, then will I make weak things become strong unto them" (Ether 12:27).

Chris shares this experience:

> This scripture, Ether 12:27, came to mean a great deal for me several years ago. I was at a point in my life when I started to feel increasingly discouraged. Despite the fact that I was achieving many good things, I felt like I needed to strengthen my commitment to the Lord and His work. As I contemplated the things I could improve in my life, I turned to the Lord in prayer. What I discovered—in terms of the comforting peace and strength from the Lord—gave me total confidence to move forward with faith. One night when praying I literally felt in my heart that the Savior knew me, forgave me of my sins, understood my challenges, and was prepared and ready to help me in a real way.

Be Led by Example

You'll find that both the scriptures and this mortal experience are filled with examples of individuals who have mastered fearless dating and have worked for great marriages. They show us that happiness in marriage is possible, and that you can make it happen. Nephi "took [a woman] to wife" (see 1 Nephi 16:7), Rachel met Jacob, and the Prophet Joseph Smith courted and married Emma. Each of these stories is different, but all have one thing in common: they each trusted in the Lord and took action.

Trusting in the Lord is easy when everything is going well and when the answers are easy to find. But what about when things are extremely difficult and there seem to be more questions than answers? No matter what you may be thinking right now about your dating future, it is possible to turn your life's question marks into exclamation points! You can create the love story that will be told about you someday and that others will gladly emulate. This story is not about being famous, or achieving greatness, or feeling superior to others. It is about serving the Lord by serving those around you.

Life is not lived in a vacuum. There are great expectations upon you not only from your parents and friends, but also from the unseen crowds, including your ancestors and future children, who cheer you on in heavenly places. There are more people who claim an interest and have a stake in your exaltation than you may ever know, so the more you take it seriously and believe in your ability to achieve, the greater your potential is in the hands of your Heavenly Father.

Now, some might ask why anyone would want to get married in the first place. No doubt you've heard that marriage is very difficult at times. You may know people in joyless marriages or have supported friends or relatives that have gone through tragic divorces. So why get married at all? Besides providing the obvious benefits of companionship, marriage allows for eternal blessings that are simply not available anywhere else. Elder Russell M. Nelson shares the following:

> Marriage is the foundry for social order, the fountain of virtue, and the foundation for eternal exaltation. Marriage has been divinely designated as an eternal and everlasting covenant (see D&C 132:19). Marriage is sanctified when it is cherished and honored in holiness. That union is not merely between husband and wife; it embraces a partnership with God (see Matthew 19:6). "Husband and wife have a solemn responsibility to love and care for each other" ("The Family: A Proclamation to the World," paragraph 6). Children born of that marital union are "an heritage of the Lord" (Psalm 127:3). Marriage is but the beginning bud of family life; parenthood is its flower. And that bouquet becomes even more beautiful when graced with grandchildren. Families may become as eternal as the kingdom of God itself (see D&C 132:19–20).[6]

Here are some reasons to prepare for marriage. The point here is to think about why the Lord instituted marriage, and how it is truly a blessing when done the Lord's way.

Marriage is great (and usually necessary) if you want to

- Enter the highest degree of the celestial kingdom (see D&C 131).
- Have joy in raising children up to the Lord (D&C 68:28).
- Always have someone to serve daily.
- Follow the Lord's command to "leave father and mother, and . . . cleave unto [your spouse] and . . . be one" (Genesis 2:24).
- Learn how to love someone deeply.
- Always have a Friday night date.
- Apply the truth that "man is not without woman, neither woman without the man" (1 Corinthians. 11:11).
- Increase honor in life through marriage (Hebrews 13:4).
- Create greater opportunities for service in the kingdom of God.
- Always have someone to kiss.
- Share protection, comfort, and support with your spouse.
- Increase your health (studies have confirmed this).
- Always have a partner in temple service.
- Read scriptures together and learn from each other.
- Always have someone with whom to play sports.
- Have an FHE with more people attending than just yourself.
- Experience greater happiness in sharing your talents with your spouse as well as others.
- Always have a dance partner.
- Not have to be a ministering angel for all eternity.
- Always have a cheerleader, and be able to cheer for someone else.
- Always have someone to enjoy ice cream and a movie with.
- Go on fun family trips together.
- Share household duties.

 We can have eternal life if we want it, but only if there is nothing else we want more.
—Elder Bruce C. Hafen

Exaltation, as outlined in the scriptures, requires a man and a woman who have individually exercised their agency to create a trilateral covenant in the temple, with each other and with Heavenly

Father. By doing so, the couple enters into the path toward godhood. This man and woman are on their way toward attaining the title and powers that Heavenly Father possesses. This is no small act. It is awesome to contemplate this wonderful blessing that Heavenly Father provides us when we choose to accept it. This divine path starts with small steps. Alma explains, "Now ye may suppose that this is foolishness in me; but behold I say unto you, that by small and simple things are great things brought to pass; and small means in many instances doth confound the wise" (Alma 37:6).

Asking someone on a date is a small thing. Attending institute is a small thing. Showering and primping are small. Speaking with clean language and strictly watching clean entertainment are small things. And all of these small things add up. We can see in the lives of great individuals how they did small things that ultimately led to eternal marriage—with enjoyable detours through successful dating.

Katy had dated lots of different guys but had very little interest in anyone in particular. It seemed like the ones she had been interested in were less interested in her, and the ones she didn't care for were ready with a ring and a temple date. She faced other obstacles as well, which included personal challenges with feelings of doubt. But throughout her years of dating, she stayed focused on what she wanted. She worked on herself, kept things in perspective, and made herself attractive in every way possible. She got an education, studied a lot, worked in areas that interested her, and stayed in shape by eating right and exercising regularly.

After several years, Katy settled down with the man of her dreams—a worthy priesthood holder named Doug who fell deeply in love with her. They are now happily married. In retrospect, Katy did the small things. In so doing, she found a man, who like Katy, possessed a testimony, a loving heart, and a beautiful future. Katy witnessed firsthand that "intelligence cleaveth unto intelligence; wisdom receiveth wisdom; truth embraceth truth; virtue loveth virtue; light cleaveth unto light; mercy hath compassion on mercy and claimeth her own; justice continueth its course and claimeth its own" (D&C 88:40).

When we interviewed renowned LDS scholar Hugh Nibley shortly before he passed away, his wife shared this experience regarding how they met:

By the time he was finished with serving in the war, and ready to go back to teaching, Hugh went to the Church offices. Brother Widtsoe, an Apostle, offered Hugh a position at Brigham Young University (BYU) and then said, "But you need to be married." So, Hugh said, "Alright, if you arrange so the first girl I meet on campus be my intended wife, I'll do it." And I was the first girl he met.

He came to BYU in June after the term had ended, and the campus was almost empty. He came looking for a room and I was working in the housing office, so he asked me for addresses. So, I was the first girl he met.

He asked me to go on a picnic with him, we took walks together, ate dinner together in the cafeteria and he asked me to marry him and we got married in September, right before fall term started.[7]

Who else but Hugh Nibley could have an experience like that? You can. No, you might not have that kind of conversation with a member of the Quorum of the Twelve, but you can have an equally effective conversation with the Lord. He will guide and direct you to your spouse. It may not happen in the timing you want it to, but it will happen.

"Wherefore, whoso believeth in God might with surety hope for a better world, yea, even a place at the right hand of God, which hope cometh of faith, maketh an anchor to the souls of men, which would make them sure and steadfast, always abounding in good works, being led to glorify God" (Ether 12:4).

• •

1. Gordon B. Hinckley, "Pillars of Truth," *Ensign*, Jan. 1994, 2.
2. Jeffrey R. Holland, "Cast Not Away Therefore Your Confidence," BYU Devotional, Mar. 2, 1999.
3. Joseph B. Wirthlin, "Life's Lessons Learned," *Ensign,* May 2007, 46.
4. Young Women and Young Men general presidencies, "Real Confidence," *New Era*, Jan. 2007, 8–10.
5. Neal A. Maxwell, "'A Brother Offended,'" *Ensign*, May 1982, 37.
6. Russell M. Nelson, "Nurturing Marriage," *Ensign*, May 2006, 36–37.
7. Hugh and Phyllis Nibley, interviewed by the authors.

Week Two Commitment: Be your best self, and follow the righteous examples of others. On a sheet of paper, write down what you feel are your strengths. Then write down 5 characteristics you would like to develop and how you will do so (for example, "I will serve someone every day to develop more charity", or "I will share my testimony with someone this week to develop greater faith"). Then work on these goals throughout the week.

Characteristics

1. _____

_____

_____

2. _____

_____

_____

3. _____

_____

_____

4. _____

_____

_____

5. _____

_____

_____

3

Prepare Effectively

Developing You in 4 B's

Regardless of your present dating prospects, you can spend this precious time of preparation developing qualities that will prepare you for marriage.—Eric B. Shumway[1]

You are now engaged in the process of preparing for a great marriage. Hopefully you are experiencing the joy that comes from successful self-improvement. During this chapter, we will dive even deeper into an exploration of what it means to become better. Be ready to stare in the mirror and smile and improve.

Eddie P. states, "You have to be the person you are looking to attract."

Shauna J. adds, "The most important thing is to work on yourself, [and] make yourself into the type of person who you would want to date. As you do that, other people will be attracted to you and want to take you out."

If you have ever baked cookies, you know that it takes specific ingredients to make them delicious. Each ingredient needs to be measured in the right proportions, or else what started as food may pop out of the oven as cardboard. In the same way, preparation for dating and marriage requires certain ingredients, the most important of which, as outlined in the scriptures, are tied to spiritual, physical, mental, and social preparation (see Luke 2:52). As you combine these ingredients in the right amounts, and bake them for the right amount of time, you will experience the resulting confidence you desire. In the following diagram, notice how being strong, social, and smart all contribute to being spiritual. In turn, your spirituality feeds each of the other respective areas.

The Dating Preparation Triangle

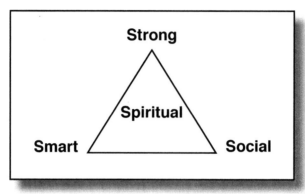

Daniel C. adds,

> Dating effectively really depends on four points. First, the core of everything is spiritual. Jesus Christ grew in stature and in wisdom and in favor with God and man. Included in that scripture are all four categories: spiritual, physical, mental, and social, all those four aspects of character. . . . For example, are you reading the scriptures, are you preparing yourself spiritually to have the kind of experiences you want to have [through] temple attendance, . . . [and] magnifying your calling? Educationally, are you pushing yourself to study and get educated? Are you exercising, staying in shape? If you want to attract a person who is healthy and in shape you have to be that first. Socially, you need to get out of your comfort zone, talk to people. Focus all your efforts on being the best you. "Perfect," is what they say in the scriptures and is the "whole you." Give your best, and people will respond.

 In the last analysis, what we are communicates far more eloquently than anything we say.—Anonymous

Be Spiritual

To be spiritual is to qualify for inspiration from heaven. Spirituality is not about having blind faith; it's about possessing active, vibrant faith that strengthens your convictions with every step you take through life.

To be spiritual is to be a prayerful person who studies the scriptures daily, keeps the commandments, magnifies callings, and attends all Church meetings. To be spiritual, a person needs to completely avoid destructive influences such as pornography, racism, gambling, and every other evil thing that offends the Spirit.

To be spiritual is to be of service to those in need and to extend a helping hand to those around you. Take responsibility to serve in a Christlike way. Have a "good Samaritan" mind-set and look for opportunities to bring people happiness and inspire others to repent and seek the Savior in their lives. Honor the priesthood. Attend the temple regularly, even if it is necessary to make sacrifices. President Thomas S. Monson related the following story:

> May we love the temple. One who did so was a devoted and faithful elderly Tahitian named Tahauri Hutihuti. Brother Hutihuti was a pearl diver from the island of Takaroa in the Taumotu Island group. Oh, how he longed to go to the temple of God! How he loved his wife! How he honored and loved his children! But the temple was beyond his reach. At that time there was no temple in the South Pacific. Then came the glorious news that a temple would be constructed in New Zealand. Carefully Brother Hutihuti prepared himself spiritually for that day. His wife did the same, as well as the children. When the time came that the New Zealand Temple was to be dedicated, old Tahauri reached beneath his bed and retrieved six hundred dollars—his life's savings accumulated throughout his forty years as a pearl diver—and gave all, that he might take his wife and his children to the temple of God in New Zealand. No sacrifice was too great. He loved the temple.[2]

In the temple, we receive a clearer perspective of the plan of happiness. The temple is the Lord's university, a place to learn how to do our life's work at each stage in our mortal existence. No other place on earth is better suited to teach us what it means and what it takes to become like our Heavenly Parents and experience the eternal happiness that they enjoy. Countless married couples report that frequent temple attendance during their dating years brought them great peace and answers to urgent prayers.

Dave K. says of his choice in an eternal companion, "She needs to be spiritual, active in church, temple worthy, and comfortable talking about the gospel. I want to feel inspired to live the gospel when I'm around her."

Abe R. adds, "I want a wife who is attractive to me, who gives her best, who wants to be a mother, who does everything she can to strengthen the family and me."

Anna B. says, "My future husband must be a Captain Moroni. That is, he has lofty goals but always seeks the kingdom of God first."

 We are what we repeatedly do. Excellence, therefore, is not an act but a habit.—Aristotle

Define your greatest values and where you are now in your spiritual journey. Commit to what you will and won't do. This is an important exercise in faith and preparation. Do it often, at least once a week. Run through an inventory of what it is you need to do to be more spiritual and what you need to stop doing. As so many successful people have, you'll find that there is always something to improve. Like the parents of the two thousand stripling warriors, who buried their weapons of war, you should be willing to bury any bad habits in your life and leave them buried forever. And like the two thousand stripling warriors, who committed to give anything to defend their families and liberties, you should be willing to adopt and maintain the best habits in your life.

Stephen G. says, "Someone with good character is someone who does what they say they'll do, when they say they'll do it. If someone commits to a level of relationship, whether that is friendship or romantic dating, then their actions follow suit with the commitments that they've made."

Jane S. says, "I'm a big fan of 'actions speak louder than words.' If someone says something, but won't back it up, I think that tells you a lot about them."

Exercise integrity. Integrity is best measured by our behavior when no one is watching. Does our private behavior vary from our public behavior? Would our behavior change if a family member, friend, or Jesus Christ were watching us? This is not to say that most of us are going to commit crimes, act dishonestly in the organizations that employ us, fornicate, or solicit an illegal drug deal. But do we spread untrue rumors about people we don't like? Do we use other peoples' possessions without asking for permission first? Do we stretch the truth to benefit ourselves?

A wise man once said, "To lie is to separate yourself from God and men." Little indiscretions often lead to bigger sins. We start to think that we are above the law or that established rules don't apply to us. Being deceitful makes it difficult to establish any sort of meaningful relationship because you will always be preoccupied with remembering what you told and to whom. If you are completely honest, you will attract others who value integrity. You will be able to establish confidence with people whom you date and court. Ultimately, when you find the one you will marry, you will have the knowledge and comfort that the covenant you enter into with that person will be one in which each person has a full commitment and dedication to making it work.

Honesty is like a mirror. No matter how hard people try, they can't change the reflection. It is what it is. They may try to cover it up with a cloth or with their hand, but the true reflection is still always there, and it will ultimately be revealed (and that may be scary for some people). Accepting it, living with it, and improving that reflection, of honesty, is what life is all about.

A foundation of honor, which we can establish in our lives by being true and faithful to our covenants, far outweighs any fame, fortune, or materialistic possessions we might obtain by leading a life devoid of integrity. We will become purified from the evils of this world and we will become like our Heavenly Father and his son Jesus Christ. "That ye may become the sons of God; that when he shall appear we shall be like him, for we shall see him as he is; that we may have this hope; that we may be purified even as he is pure" (Moroni 7:48).

 The greatest battles fought are in the silent chambers of your own soul.— President David O. McKay

Brother Steve DeVore, CEO of SyberVision, said,

"Maintain your spiritual habits in scripture study, personal prayer, and service. There, you create a vitality and energy. From a competitive point of view, it sets you apart. From a learning perspective, I look at my mission. I had to learn the world's most difficult language. I didn't think I had the intellect to do it. It was acquired through a lot of hard work and prayer. If you can do that, you can do anything. Look at your mission as a source of encouragement and strength. If you have fulfilled a mission, anything is possible. Apply that sense of breakthrough to everything you do."[3]

Attend the temple as often your circumstances permit. This one habit will strengthen your spiritual power in indescribable ways. Making the temple an anchor in your life will help you face life's storms with greater resolve. Prepare well for the temple, and as you attend, ponder on the Savior's sacrifice for you.

Be Smart

> " " ... Resolve now, while you are young, that you will get all of the education you can. We live in a highly competitive age, and it will only grow worse. Education is the key that will unlock the door of opportunity.—Gordon B. Hinckley[4]

Be smart and enhance your education. Go to college or trade school or take skills classes to increase your abilities and income. Develop your mind by reading good books, challenging yourself with new problems, and working on your talents. Although the Internet has succeeded in bringing seemingly unlimited information to the world, there still remains no substitute for a good book. Make learning a life-long endeavor and set a specific plan for what books you will read this year, focusing on those that will empower you in different ways. If you have an interest in political science, for example, read about it. If your opinions are particularly strong in one area, read the opposing view, so you can be better equipped to articulate your position against it.

When we interviewed successful author Stephen R. Covey, who wrote *The Seven Habits of Highly Effective People*, he said, "Develop many, many skills and keep enlarging your repertoire. I try to study two hours every day right now. I'm reading several books every week. If you keep yourself constantly learning and growing, it keeps your own material alive, and you never want to retire. Retirement is the sickest notion there is."[5]

Brian C. says, "When you see a girl who knows how to work hard and pushes herself to get good grades or progress at her work and education, that's attractive. It says something about who she is. Work defines a person."

Julie S. adds, "I like to see someone who has ambition, and who works hard. Even if someone isn't extremely intelligent, as long as he has ambition and the desire to work hard, that makes me interested."

As you pursue work and a career, it is vital that you do what you love. Being enslaved by your job is not something anyone should volunteer for, yet there are millions of people who hate their jobs. Doing what you enjoy will reflect in doing a great job—be it business, art, science, teaching, or anything else. Simply put, doing something boring over and over, eight hours a day, five days a week, for the rest of your life is not the optimum path to happiness. Choose a career where you can contribute and love it at the same time. Of course, this doesn't mean you ought to look for a job that will pay you to sit and watch Disney movies or engineer paper airplanes all day. A career, even when you love it, is still work. But when you do love it, work becomes better defined as fun.

How do you figure out what you love? Experiment. Ask friends, family, and other trusted individuals that see you in action and know your interests. Consider what you think about most. If you think about teaching a concept or idea all the time, maybe its time for you to consider teaching; if you are always wondering how biological phenomena interact on a molecular level, maybe working in a lab would be your best bet.

People who hate their jobs are not the most cheery people around. You owe it to yourself, your future family, the Savior, and the world to do what you enjoy. Remember, however, that you don't have to—nor may you be able to—jump into your "dream job" right this minute. You will probably need to prepare yourself by getting key work experience and education. Just remember to always stay focused on your goal.

Ryan Woodward, animator and storyboard artist for films like *Spider-Man 2* is clearly someone who loves his job. He said, "I share my secret to success: First, live the gospel. Second, follow your dreams. If you do that, you'll be successful. Your dreams may change, but that is probably a result of living the gospel. Your heart will open to the inspiration [of] where the Lord wants you to go."[6]

Be Strong

"Cease to be idle; cease to be unclean; cease to find fault one with another; cease to sleep longer than is needful; retire to thy bed early, that ye may not be weary; arise early, that your bodies and your minds may be invigorated" (D&C 88:124).

Be physically fit. Confidence is impossible to achieve when you're so tired that you doze off during a date. So get sufficient rest. According to scientific research, the best hours for sleep are generally between 11:00 p.m. and 1:00 a.m., so, be sure to be in bed by 11:00 p.m., or, by very rare exception, midnight at the latest.

 No matter who you are, no matter what you do, you absolutely, positively do have the power to change.
—Bill Phillips

Another key to being fit is eating well. Limit the junk food. Think of your body as a high-powered jet. It only runs properly on high quality jet fuel. That means putting the Pop Tarts and Twinkies where they belong—in the trash! The ideal way is to eat mid-sized quantities of quality grains, high-protein foods, and fruits and vegetables. Don't overeat. Studies show that people who overeat consistently will gain weight and die. Of course, they don't die right away, but essentially what they're telling their body when they stuff it full is, "I don't have much time left at all here on earth, so let's eat all we can, while we can." That kind of food storage isn't the kind the prophet is recommending.

The body has certain limitations. Just like a jet flies a lot better when it is not overfilled with folks hanging in the cargo bins and laying over the tops of chairs or on top of the wings, the body handles life and progresses much better when it's not "over capacity."

Remember to be active. Nephi was "large in stature" for a reason. He walked a lot (to Jerusalem and back more than once) and he lifted heavy plates frequently. Try to focus on key areas in your exercise. First, exercise two to three times per week by doing cardio, such as running, biking, walking, or jogging to promote heart health. Second, exercise at least once a week by playing sports or doing yoga, martial arts, or other aerobics to stay agile and flexible. Third, exercise two to three times per week by doing some kind of strength training like weight lifting, sit-ups, or push-ups to build muscle.

Dane W. states, "I can't be going after all the supermodels because I'm not one. I can't be going after things that I don't have. And I can't expect things that I can't contribute. I can't expect a girl that I want to date to be all these great and wonderful things, if I can't be that for her."

We read in *For the Strength of Youth*, "Choose righteousness and happiness, no matter what your circumstances. Take responsibility for the choices you make. Develop your abilities and talents, and use them for good. Avoid idleness and be willing to work hard."[7]

Work hard at everything you do. The need to work is one of the most fundamental principles Heavenly Father has given us for our spiritual and physical well-being. In the Garden of Eden, God told Adam, "By the sweat of thy face shalt thou eat bread, until thou shalt return unto the ground" (Moses 4:25). Think of these questions you may want to ask yourself about those whom you are dating:

- Does this person have goals? Can I see that this person is preparing to accomplish them?
- Does this person have any ambition in life?
- What motivates this person?
- Does this person's example increase my desire to be a better person and work hard in my own life?

If your answers to these questions are either "no" or "I don't know," you may want to rethink whether pursuing a relationship with that person is actually worth it.

By accomplishing goals through hard work, we develop the kind of discipline and self-control that the Lord expects of His people. Discipline and self-control help us resist the buffetings of Satan in our personal lives and strengthen us in our efforts to build the kingdom of God on the earth. We can then focus and prioritize on what truly is our most important work.

When we interviewed LDS author and former member of the general Relief Society presidency Chieko Okasaki, she shared the following experience about her husband:

> My husband and I were called in 1968 to open the second mission in Japan. We finished our mission in 1971 and returned to Denver. Although my husband didn't have a job for six months, he deserves a lot of credit. In the six months he went to Catholic charities to get an entry-level social work job, to Kmart to get a warehouse worker job. He went to the county and finally earned a job in social work. He was grateful for the work and in six month's time the director retired and gave my husband's name to the county. He became the director. If you do your best, the Lord is always on your side.[8]

When we interviewed former astronaut and senator Jake Garn, he shared the following:

> When I was running for senator in 1974, I knocked on over 50,000 doors. I believe in the incredible importance of working hard and being educated, and even much more today with the speed of technological change. That is key in any type of profession or skilled labor. You must be educated to compete. It's amazing, if you have those attitudes, what you can achieve in life. I look back and say, "How did little Jake Garn get to do all of these things?" I think the major factor was that, while I could not specifically plan for everything I have done in my life, when the opportunity came, I could stand up and say, "I can do that."[9]

Keep your living space clean. Have you ever walked into an apartment and felt like you were entering a hazardous war zone? It isn't a pleasant experience. The cleaning habits that you develop and live by while you are single will continue in your dating, and ultimately in your marriage. Can you imagine being married, having a few kids, and living in an apartment or house that is a complete disaster?

Clarissa T. mentions: "Be your best self. Love life and take care of yourself. Grow close to God and maintain order in your life. If you don't have yourself in order, you may try to get in a relationship that is chaotic."

One of the great benefits of exercising high levels of personal cleanliness is the way it makes us feel. When the environment in which we reside is clean, it makes us feel positive and happy. We don't have to deal with the distractions that disorganization brings into our lives. When we are in a good frame of mind, we are freed to be our best selves and to focus more on helping others with their burdens.

Alisson O. says, "Develop into the type of person you want to live with, someone who isn't too demanding or difficult to be around. Be a pleasant person, and work on improving yourself. Every dating situation you have is an opportunity to teach you how to be a better person."

Stay out of debt. Modern-day prophets have repeatedly counseled us on the need for us to be self-sufficient and debt-free, with the exception of going into debt for education or the purchase of a modest home. As we seek to provide for our families and practice financial responsibility, our confidence will grow. As we implement a "provident living" lifestyle, we will experience the freedom that comes from living lives of discipline. As we free ourselves from the bondage caused by living outside our means, we will be able to devote more of ourselves to building the kingdom of God on earth.

Save your money. With each check you earn, pay tithing, and then put away a certain percentage for your savings, as little as ten or twenty percent. In other words, pay the Lord, and then pay yourself. This will slowly build a reserve for you and your family in the future, and you will be more financially prepared to accomplish your goals.

Be Social

"And that same sociality which exists among us here will exist among us there, only it will be coupled with eternal glory, which glory we do not now enjoy" (D&C 130:2).

We are social beings. Spending every night glued to a computer or television screen is not only unattractive, it's also unhealthy. It's the equivalent of spending all of one's quality time with a toaster. No matter how much love you give to that toaster, it's never going to give you back anything, except toasted bread. It's just that simple.

What does it mean to be social? Go to church, institute, sports functions, ward and stake activities, and dances. Go out of your way to meet and befriend new people. Taking the time to get to know others will open doors and bless lives. So often, single adults complain that they can't seem to find the "right person," but they are often unwilling to go to the right places to find the right person. Being in the right place is one of the greatest keys to finding the right person.

Regarding the benefits of being social, Trisha B. says, "I think most of my successful dating experiences have come through people whom I have met on my own. When I want a guy to be more interested in me, I make myself more available. A lot of guys talk about girls who stand around in groups and how intimidating that can be. I go out of my way to be friendly."

Sandra L. adds, "I think by hanging out in the places you like, like institute and dances, you will find people who have similar interests and have things in common with you. So I think just by going about your everyday life, you will meet those people with similar values."

Scott W. describes asking out girls in social settings:

> When you meet somebody, usually in a social situation, whether it be in the ward, a party, a fireside, a social gathering, don't ask them out immediately. Focus first on getting to know the person. Then let the social setting follow your intention of getting to know them. When one voids oneself of romantic intention as much as possible, then the tone and how you approach people is completely different. Rather than predatory, it is one of genuine interest.
>
> Build good relationships, even if they aren't necessarily good dating relationships. Build good relationships with everyone around you. Better relationships with your parents, siblings, and friends. Build new friendships by being outgoing and genuinely caring about other people. As you do this, you will eventually find someone with whom you are compatible and for whom you're willing to sacrifice.

Referring to a girl's power to initiate dating opportunities, Ray says, "Girls know the game all too well. They know how to make it easy for you to ask them out. If she comes up next to me and starts talking to me (for example sitting next to me), not being too forward, but making it easier to get to know her, that helps the whole process."

Set Goals

Rodney Brady, CEO of Deseret Management Corporation said, "When I was a young man, I set goals categorized in eight groupings—spiritual, family, professional, educational, financial, cultural and creative, athletic and physical fitness, and miscellaneous goals. Among some of the goals in my professional life were the following: Some day I wanted to run a major corporation, which I have. I wanted to serve as a leader of a major academic institution, which I have. I wanted to serve in high level government service, which I have."[10]

· ·

1.   Eric B. Shumway, "Preparing Yourself for Marriage," *Ensign*, Oct. 2008, 54.

2.   Thomas S. Monson, *Be Your Best Self* (Salt Lake City: Deseret Book, 1979), 54.

3.   Steve DeVore, interviewed by the authors.

4.   Gordon B. Hinckley, "Let Virtue Garnish Thy Thoughts Unceasingly,"

Ensign, May 2007, 115.

5. Steven R. Covey, interviewed by the authors.
6. Ryan Woodward, interviewed by the authors.
7. *For the Strength of Youth: Fulfilling Our Duty to God* (Salt Lake City: Intellectual Reserve, 2001), 5.
8. Chieko Okasaki, interviewed by the authors.
9. Jake Garn, interviewed by the authors.
10. Rodney Brady, interviewed by the authors.

Week Three Commitment: Set personal goals for becoming more spiritual, smart, strong, and social. Write on a sheet of paper a goal for each area, including specific things you need to do to achieve each goal (for example, "spiritual: read the Book of Mormon for 30 minutes daily; smart: spend 30 minutes daily developing a new talent; strong: run 2 miles daily, social: go to institute weekly"). Make these goals into habits, and check your progress every few weeks or so.

Goal

Spiritual

1. _____

2. _____

3. _____

Smart

1. _____

2. _____

3. _____

Strong

1. _____

2. _____

3. _____

Social

1. _____

2. _____

3. _____

Part 2:

A Righteous Foundation

4

Date with Purpose

Writing your Love Story

How beautiful is youth; how bright it gleams, with its illusions, aspirations, dreams. Book of beginnings, story without end; each maid a heroine, each man a friend.—Henry Wadsworth Longfellow

With your goals set in all the key categories, you are now ready to set your sights on dating with purpose. This may seem like an obvious discussion to have, but we will have it anyway. In fact, don't be surprised if this chapter becomes a personal favorite for you as we talk about why dating is so important and how to make it important.

Keep Your Eye on Exaltation

Dating with the right purpose in mind is a lot like driving a car. There's not one "perfect" way to drive a car, but there are many wrong ways. Driving into oncoming traffic or into a tree, for example, are wrong ways to drive. It is also wrong to drive without knowing where you're going. That is, if you want to get to Omaha, Nebraska from where you are, you shouldn't just accelerate onto a random freeway going any direction. You could end up in California, Kentucky, or even Mesquite, Nevada. To get to your destination, you're going to need a map—not just any map either, but a current one. Dating is no different.

 My advice to you is get married: if you find a good wife you'll be happy; if not, you'll become a philosopher. —Socrates

Dating with a purpose provides perspective for the journey. Always keep in mind the purpose of exaltation. Yes, you may—and most likely will—need to date a lot of people before you discover who you're really looking for. But as you move forward, you should at least have a good sense of why you're doing what you're doing. Otherwise, you can end up far from where you want to be. Derek, for example, constantly dated girls he had very little interest in marrying. Yes, he was physically attracted to them and he enjoyed their personalities. However, when asked if those he dated were the type of women he wanted to be his wife and the mother of his children, he responded, "No. Not even. I'm just dating them for fun."

Derek's story is, unfortunately, fairly common. However, someone who follows his footsteps may find that the road that leads to momentary pleasure often leads to eternal wifelessness. The better road, recommended by the Brethren, is to be serious about the people you date. This means that you should be thinking in terms of this being a person who you and the Lord can approve of. After all, when everything is said and done, you will be the one living with the person you choose to marry for all eternity. Remember that you marry who you date.

Throughout the Church, more young adult men are making the mistake of just hanging out instead of really dating. Says one study, "The top three factors to delay marriage for BYU students, according to this study are the fear of making a mistake, the need for emotional maturity and the fear of responsibility. In the 1950s, the era of the traditional family, people got married young—men at 22 and women at 20. . . . Since the '50s, marriage age has increased, creating a larger gap of single people pursuing education and professions."[1]

You daters of this generation definitely have your challenges, but certainly the Lord expects this generation to be great, one that moves forward as each of you prepare your marriage and family for the Second Coming of the Savior. Facing future responsibly—without fear of making mistakes and while exercising emotional maturity—will prepare you for what you need to do. And yet, some of the problems you currently face are surely related to the times.

One such problem is that many young adults of this generation are either not taking marriage seriously or are avoiding it entirely. What is the solution to this marriage avoidance issue? What can be done to help young people realize their most important responsibility in life?

Elder Bruce R. McConkie offered this counsel:

> When we as Latter-day Saints talk about marriage, we are talking about a holy, celestial order. We are talking about a system out of which can grow the greatest love, joy, peace, happiness, and serenity known to humankind. We are talking about creating a family unit that has the potential of being everlasting and eternal, a family unit where a man and a wife can go on in that relationship to all eternity. . . . We are talking about creating a unit more important than the Church, more important than any organization that exists on earth or in heaven, a unit out of which exaltation and eternal life grow, and when we talk about eternal life, we are talking about the kind of life that God our Heavenly Father lives.[2]

Throughout history, men and women have left legacies in their work, but no legacy is greater than that of being part of a blessed marriage and bearing righteous posterity that can positively influence a struggling world. Clearly, we need to make such a legacy our priority. In the movie *Legacy*, one character notes, "Remember that with pain, suffering, and patience, God also allows us joy." When we interviewed Academy Award–winning filmmaker Kieth Merrill, director of the film *Legacy*, he said, "Marry the right person. Prepare. And remember your temple covenants. Don't ever compromise. Make the important decisions only once."[3]

Joseph R. describes dating when he says, "The whole point of dating is to find somebody whom you can trust enough, confide in enough, and be compatible enough with that you will let this person into your world, where you can expose the aspects of your life to this person that you may not want other people to know about. The first date is the most crucial in trying to progress down that road."

Choose the Right Date

> "And the Messiah cometh in the fulness of time, that he may redeem the children of men from the fall. And because that they are redeemed from the fall they have become free forever, knowing good from evil; to act for themselves and not to be acted upon, save it be by the punishment of the law at the great and last day, according to the commandments which God hath given.
>
> Wherefore, men are free according to the flesh; and call things are given them which are expedient unto man. And they are free

to choose liberty and eternal life, through the great Mediator of all men, or to choose captivity and death, according to the captivity and power of the devil; for he seeketh that all men might be miserable like unto himself" (2 Nephi 2:26–27).

Through the Atonement of Jesus Christ, we have been given the blessed gift of agency. It is the freedom to choose the right, to make the best decisions, and to therefore be blessed eternally. What are the right decisions in dating? Here are some examples of both wrong and right choices.

Some Wrong Choices

I won't ask out many people because I fear rejection.

Why? Being rejected is never a reason to give up hope. In fact, almost every happily married person experienced some sort of rejection in dating. Rejection is difficult to face, but it may be very helpful in guiding you along to the right person.

I only go to the movies on a first date.

Why? Spending two hours together in silence as you watch a movie is not conducive to conversation. It often leads quickly down "No Second Date Road."

I'd make sure to be totally alone with my date from the get-go.

Why? Church leaders recommend being in public places together, and not alone in places like a parked car, because it can lead to serious sin that was completely preventable. Good intentions, no matter how good, don't go well with potentially bad situations.

I date solely to have fun. Looking for marriage is too much pressure.

Why? Dating should be fun—that is a fact. But dating only for pleasure, without thinking of the greater purpose of marriage can lead to monumental acts of stupidity, like marrying the wrong person, just because you became emotionally attached.

I only "hang out" in groups. Dating is too stressful.

Why? A happy marriage is the product of real dating. Dating requires one-on-one time that is planned, paid for, and paired off, in which both people can share quality time and learn to selflessly serve the other.

I only date over the Internet. I can get to know the person just as well, and I don't have to worry about face-to-face rejection.

Why? Internet dating was never designed to replace real dating. Even if people meet each other online, they still need to date in real life. Don't go giving your heart to someone in cyberspace only to find out that in real life they have the appetite of a rhino and only shower during winter solstice. Also, there are many predatory people who shop for victims on the Internet, so normal individuals like you need to be very, *very* careful with Internet dating.

Some Right Choices

I'll ask anyone out if I'm really interested. Sure, I may be rejected, but it's not the end of the world.

Great attitude! Rejection is a fact of life. You will probably be rejected sometimes. And that's okay. But you will be accepted many more times, statistically speaking. So, go for it! Ask away.

I like to go on fun, simple first dates where we have plenty of opportunity to talk and get to know each other.

Great idea! The first date is all about breaking the ice and learning who this person is so you can check to see if you're actually compatible.

I prefer to stay in public places with my date. It's safer, and hey, I get to show off the fact that I'm actually on a date!

Great idea! This will keep you safe, morally speaking. This means going to activities where there are always other people around, at least in the early stages of dating.

Remember Responsibility

Responsibility is a big word with big meaning. It takes great effort to be responsible. Being responsible is far more than just taking out the trash when asked. It extends to accepting accountability for creating your own righteous success in the world, predicated on the principles of the restored gospel. President Gordon B. Hinckley quoted Joseph F. Smith in saying, "No man can be saved and exalted in the kingdom of God without the woman, and no woman can reach perfection and exaltation in the kingdom of God, alone. . . . God instituted marriage in the beginning. He made man in His own image and likeness, male and female, and in their creation it was designed that they should be united together in sacred bonds of marriage, and one is not perfect without the other."[4]

Prophets have always testified of the joy and power of a righteous marriage, and the great influence righteous marriage has on eternity. Surely the Lord wants everyone to seek for and eventually enjoy this great blessing. Whether every single person will marry in this life is not part of our discussion. The Lord, being just and merciful, will surely bless each of His children who do all they can for a happy, eternal marriage, in this life or in the eternities. President Gordon B. Hinckley said, "Surely no one reading the scriptures, both ancient and modern, can doubt the divine concept of marriage. The sweetest feelings of life, the most generous and satisfying impulses of the human heart, find expression in a marriage that stands pure and unsullied above the evil of the world. Such a marriage, I believe, is the desire—the hoped-for, the longed-for, the prayed-for desire—of men and women everywhere."[5]

We read in the book of Genesis that after slaying Abel, Cain asked the Lord if he was his brother's keeper (Genesis 4:9). The answer for him, as well as for all of us, is a resounding "Yes!" Life is not an individual sport. Though we each have our individual agency and accountability, we also know that the Lord expects us to help those around us to reach their true potential through our love, support, and example. Likewise, a lone individual cannot reach the highest degree of the celestial kingdom unless that individual enters and keeps the new and everlasting covenant of marriage.

Take responsibility now, in whatever you are doing, to prove to the Lord that you will be responsible in handling any future stewardship. Remember that your thoughts, words, and behaviors have a direct impact on others. This willingness to take responsibility for the assignments and relationships that you have been given while in mortality is a true sign of maturity.

Speaking of his responsibilities, Brandon Doman, former Brigham Young University and San Francisco 49ers quarterback, said:

My family is the most important blessing that I have. They come first. My career comes second. If my career ever steps in front of the well-being of my family, I won't do it. I have the goal of having a big family and supporting them in their dreams. The many great lessons and habits that you learned by living the gospel were acquired for a reason. Don't lose them (see 2 Nephi 31:20 and D&C 90:24). Focus your life on building the kingdom and nothing else. Rise in the morning with your eyes placed solely on helping our Father in Heaven bring to pass the immortality and eternal life of man (Moses 1:39).[6]

When you are dedicating your life to performing your responsibilities, others with similar self-discipline will be attracted to you. As you show the Lord that you are motivated to fulfill the responsibilities in your life, you will receive more opportunities.

We can never feel like we've learned everything there is to know about the gospel and about the Lord. We need to hunger for righteousness throughout our lives by accepting and magnifying the responsibilities given to us. As we do this, the Lord will bless us with further instruction, and we will progress on the path that leads to Him.

Being a responsible disciple of Jesus Christ is our foremost obligation in this life. President James E. Faust shared the following: "For most of us . . . what is required is not to die for the Church but to live for it. For many, living a Christlike life every day may be even more difficult than laying down one's life. . . . Many think that the price of discipleship is too costly and too burdensome. For some, it involves giving up too much. But the cross is not as heavy as it appears to be. Through obedience we acquire much greater strength to carry it."[7]

Search the Scriptures

In the midst of dating difficulties, many people turn to whatever source may give them the quickest, most easily available answers. Unfortunately, many of those answers are found in the world's teachings and do not provide the spiritual power necessary for people to achieve their divine destiny. This relying on "the arm of flesh" is a fast track to terrible tragedy. Fortunately, the Lord has revealed His word to us so that we can be guided in these potentially confusing times. The scriptures provide all the answers you need in every aspect of life—especially dating and courtship. One man said that the Book of Mormon: Another Testament of Jesus Christ ought to have an additional subtitle on the cover that reads, "A Guide for Preparing for Marriage." It is true that the Book of Mormon helps us through every stage of life, from entering Primary, serving a mission, getting married, or raising Primary children of our own.

The scriptures are filled with powerful words of truth that you can't find anywhere else. This being the case, how should you go about searching the scriptures? Is there one best way for studying the scriptures? Yes and no. There are certain keys to scripture study that will make it effective for you. Set aside a consistent time every day to search the scriptures for thirty minutes, especially the Book of Mormon. Pray for the guidance of the Spirit, and write down the promptings that come to you. How you study, whether it's chapter by chapter or topic by topic, is something you can decide for yourself.

Many happy people report that the scriptures have offered the very answers they needed exactly when they needed them. One young man, Danny, was interested in dating a certain young woman, Janae, but had some concerns. She was everything he ever wanted, but Danny didn't know how to go about courting her. If Danny didn't do something different from the other guys who were pursuing Janae, he would likely not create enough interest for her to want to date him. After turning to friends and family for suggestions, Danny wisely sought answers in the scriptures, particularly the Book of Mormon. He prayed and began to read. Soon Danny realized he felt like Nephi. Nephi was instructed by the Lord to build a boat, an immense task unlike anything Nephi had done before. Danny found confidence in Nephi's story, knowing that he too had embarked on a great mission from the Lord to arrive at his own promised land.

After demonstrating interest in Janae by talking to her, getting to know her better, and then asking her out, Danny was ready to keep dating her. But Janae was being courted by several eligible guys who were just as interested in her as Danny was. Danny again turned to the scriptures. This time, he joined Captain Moroni. He noticed the spiritual power and presence of Captain Moroni, whose heart was filled with gratitude, and whose desire was to serve his people with perfect love and righteousness. Danny set about to do the same thing in his life. He looked for opportunities to serve his family, friends, home teaching families, even strangers, and Janae. As a result, Janae started to take more interest in him. "Maybe he's the right type of guy for me," Janae thought to herself.

As time went on, Danny found that Janae's interest in him seemed to be waning. He wondered if he should give up or start over with someone else. Something in him told him to carry on. Remembering Captain Moroni's fearlessness in the face of threats of danger from evil approaching armies, Danny endeavored to be courageous in the face of his own fears. He didn't allow any negative thoughts to plague his mind. In fact, he only focused on the positive kind of thinking that would inspire him to make something great happen in his life. Like Captain Moroni preparing for war against his enemies, Danny made the preparations necessary to fight for Janae's love. When the moment was right, he brought her some flowers. She happily received them.

Danny and Janae started dating regularly. Danny read about Helaman's two thousand stripling warriors, who were exactly obedient to the Lord's commandments, and Danny confirmed his own desire to be totally obedient. Danny was careful about keeping his dating standards high by planning dates in public places and avoiding any passionate kissing. Danny took the lead in being rigid at following the rules of the Lord's Spirit. As a result, Danny and Janae experienced enjoyable, wholesome dating.

From her point of view, Janae was convinced that Danny was a great guy, but she felt she needed a more thorough investigation of the situation by spending more time with Danny, while still dating other guys for comparison. She stayed focused on getting guidance from Heavenly Father by praying daily and reading her scriptures. One day, while pondering her dating efforts, Janae wanted to know whether she should spend more or less time with Danny. She prayed, opened the Book of Mormon, and read in Alma 32 where Alma compares faith to a seed. She considered the challenge Alma gave his listeners to take care to nourish the seed, and that if it were a good seed it would grow and create powerful, good feelings. Alma also cautioned the people to be careful not to neglect the seed because neglect would prevent the seed's growth. Janae realized at that moment that her dating relationships were each seeds that she could either focus on or ignore. Each seed's growth depended on her efforts, the guy's efforts, and the help of the Lord. Truly, it was a matter of hoping for "things not seen" (see Alma 32:21).

Janae decided that she really liked Danny the most out of all the guys she was dating, and would channel her efforts in nourishing that relationship "seed." So she called Danny more frequently, invited him to activities, and complimented him whenever possible. As she did this, her feelings for Danny grew until she decided to date him exclusively.

Meanwhile, Danny felt a great increase in excitement after he and Janae started holding hands and seeing each other regularly—several times each week. As time went on, Danny became more and more concerned as his feelings for Janae grew stronger. He wanted to ensure that he would always demonstrate respect and total virtue to her and himself. Danny also wanted to maintain a sense of spontaneity in demonstrating his interest in Janae. He opened his scriptures one night, after thinking about these very issues, and read in the third chapter of 1 Nephi. Danny saw how Nephi obeyed the Lord by going to get the plates with his brothers. He read further in the chapter and discovered an even greater truth: when his plans to get the plates failed, and his brothers were trying to convince him to return to their father, Nephi stuck with his original decision to be obedient to the Lord. In the same way, Danny recommitted to the Lord to be totally, 100 percent obedient to His commandment of the law of chastity, even as Danny became more serious in dating.

Danny never regretted his decision to be totally chaste, even though he knew people who justified lying down on a couch together or engaging in passionate kissing. Danny knew that those people might be experiencing momentary pleasure, but they were not truly happy in their observance of Heavenly Father's commandments. Nor did Danny regret his decision to do all he could to achieve his objective of an eternal marriage, just as Nephi did everything in his power to do all that the Lord commanded him to do. Danny stuck with his plan to court Janae by being consistently kind, caring, spiritual, and fun. He never stopped showing interest in listening to her and spent his time doing memorable, entertaining, and uplifting activities. After several months, Danny and Janae both realized they were falling in love.

As they spent time together month after month and moved closer and closer to engagement and marriage, Janae started to experience doubts. She was still relatively young. Should she limit her options by focusing on one man with whom she should spend the majority of her time? Was she ready to be committed to someone in this way? Again, Janae turned to the scriptures. She read the experience of the brother of Jared who was tasked with the overwhelming challenge of bringing large groups of people across immense oceans. She saw how he was unsure of how they would provide air and light on the trip. Janae recognized that she was also undertaking an extremely challenging task in her life and that she needed the vital comfort of breathing easy and feeling God's light during her journey.

Janae read about the brother of Jared having a conversation with the Lord, questioning the Lord about these important problems. She was amazed how straightforward the Lord was with the brother of Jared. The Lord told him that they could put air holes in the top and bottom of each vessel, and they could unstop them for air at certain times. Janae felt that the Lord was telling her that He had a plan to get her air. That is, she could ultimately decide for herself whatever she wanted, and the Lord would get her the oxygen—or success—she desired. Janae thanked the Lord for this wonderful insight and then continued reading.

Janae wondered about the light that was needed in the ships. The brother of Jared brought the problem before the Lord, and the Lord didn't tell him what to do; the Lord only told him what wouldn't work. The Lord said that if they lit a fire it would burn the boat up. Then the Lord left things up to the brother of Jared. In the same way, Janae had a decision to make that only she could make. But like the brother of Jared, she could strive to make the right choice and enjoy more or less light based on that decision. Of course, Janae knew that Danny was not the only good returned missionary in the world with whom she could spend the rest of eternity. She also knew she would be happy no matter what decision she made regarding her relationship with Danny.

The brother of Jared found sixteen stones and asked the Lord to touch them so they could provide light in the ships. Janae wrote down her list of "Sixteen Stones," or sixteen things that mattered most to her, and then she brought her list to the Lord through prayer, and asked for His guidance regarding how her values fit with her potential future relationship with Danny. Janae felt the Lord's Spirit prompt her to continue dating Danny.

During this time, Danny was feeling somewhat frustrated. By spending most of his time with Janae, he was spending less time with his brothers and friends. He felt torn because he wanted to better balance his time among everyone he cared about, especially Janae. Again, Danny turned to the scriptures and prayed. He read about the ongoing wars between the Nephites and the Lamanites, and how the Nephites were blessed only when they turned to the Lord and relied on his power. Danny found that as he planned with the Lord's inspiration, not relying on the arm of flesh, he could set his priorities effectively, and balance his time better.

As they continued to spend time together, Janae and Danny felt stronger feelings for each other. Again, Janae started to get concerned. Were they spending too much time together? Would Danny propose to her soon and would she be ready with an answer? All of these thoughts and more raced through her head. Janae told Danny that she needed some time away from him to think. Of course, Danny didn't like this. He felt like things were going great, so it only made sense for them to keep moving forward.

Struggling for several days without seeing or speaking with Janae, Danny became more confused. Should he call her and tell her that he needed to see her? Or should he just wait for her to call? Whatever Danny decided could make all the difference for success or failure in his relationship. His dad suggested that he wait a few more days before calling her. His mom advised that he send her flowers and then give her a call the next day. His friends told him to forget about her and spend time with them, finding other girls.

During this time, Danny continued to search his scripture, and studied the experience of the Nephites who fought against the Gadianton robbers under Gidgiddoni's guidance. As the robbers hid in the mountains, some of the Nephites suggested they should go and attack them in their hiding places. But Gidgiddoni warned against it. He and Lachoneus recommended that they gather together in one place and build a stronghold of people with all their possessions, so they did. When the robbers came down from their hiding places, they found deserted cities that they could not destroy because no one was there. Then, as the robbers converged to attack the people of Nephi, they were greatly disappointed, because the Nephites were grouped into one powerful unit.

Danny took great comfort in this experience, knowing that if he pursued Janae with vigor, chasing her from place to place, he would likely lose her. But if he focused on strengthening himself, building his confidence, and achieving his goals, and waited for Janae to come to him, he would more likely be successful. After waiting a grueling week and half of not hearing from Janae, Danny could not stand it any longer. He had to do something. But he knew that according to the Lord, "something" meant "waiting." So, Danny waited. Suddenly, Janae called Danny and told him that she wanted to start seeing him again and that the time away from him was exactly what she needed for her to realize she always wanted to be with him. Danny and Janae soon got engaged, later got sealed in the temple, and now have four beautiful children.

As the experience of Danny and Janae illustrates, the scriptures provide incredible power. Through them, you can achieve insights and inspiration in the exact moments when they matter most.

Do What Is in Your Power to Do

One mistake that singles often make is to worry about things over which they have no control. National crises, others' perception of you, and even the individual agency of your date are things you can't control. And yet, so many singles constantly think about these situations. One young man confessed to having thought for over sixty-two hours straight about whether a girl he'd gone out with a few nights previous really liked him! Running a problem through your head for which you have no possible solution is like a monkey trying to fly—no matter how much effort the monkey exerts, it just won't change the situation. It is true that sometimes you can influence things, and it is true that there are often more of these situations than we might think. But it is also true that there are some things that we simply cannot change or control.

The human mind is only capable of one thought at any given moment in time. If that thought is one regarding something you cannot control, then you are dedicating precious brainpower and faith to a pointless effort. Do what is in your power to do.

After being confined in jail, unable to lead the people of God or see his family, Joseph realized he still had power to write them and encourage them with these words, "Therefore, dearly beloved brethren, let us cheerfully do all things that lie in our power; and then may we stand still, with the utmost assurance, to see the salvation of God, and for his arm to be revealed" (D&C 123:17).

1. Angela M. Fischer, "Twixters Not Ready to Grow Up," *Daily Universe,* June 20, 2005. Results from a study conducted by Richard McClendon, associate director of Brigham Young University's Office of Institutional Assessment and Analysis.
2. Bruce R. McConkie, "Celestial Marriage," *New Era*, 12 June 1978, 12.
3. Kieth Merrill, interviewed by the author.
4. Gordon B. Hinckley, "What God Hath Joined Together," *Ensign*, May 1991, 71.
5. Ibid.
6. Brandon Doman, interviewed by the authors.
7. James E, Faust, "Discipleship," *Ensign*, Nov. 2006, 22.

Week Four Commitment: Write down, in one sentence, your purpose in dating. (For example, "I am dating to select a spouse that I am attracted to, enjoy spending time with, and want to be with for eternity.")

My Purpose in Dating

_____

_____

_____

_____

_____

_____

_____

_____

_____

_____

_____

_____

_____

_____

_____

5
Date Right

Changing the "Hang out" to the "Go out"

Men, if you have returned from your mission and you are still following the boy-girl patterns you were counseled to follow when you were 15, it is time for you to grow up. Gather your courage and look for someone to pair off with. Start with a variety of dates with a variety of young women, and when that phase yields a good prospect, proceed to courtship. It's marriage time. That is what the Lord intends for His young adult sons and daughters. Men have the initiative, and you men should get on with it. If you don't know what a date is, perhaps this definition will help. I heard it from my eighteen-year-old granddaughter. A "date" must pass the test of three p's: (1) planned ahead, (2) paid for, and (3) paired off.

Young women, resist too much hanging out, and encourage dates that are simple, inexpensive, and frequent. Don't make it easy for young men to hang out in a setting where you women provide the food. Don't subsidize freeloaders. An occasional group activity is OK, but when you see men who make hanging out their primary interaction with the opposite sex, I think you should lock the pantry and bolt the front door. —Elder Dallin H Oaks[1]

Dating is a lot less complicated than some people think. But it can be miserable, or at the very least, painfully boring, if done improperly. Countless young ladies have horror stories of spending hours with someone, doing something totally uninteresting. Effective dating is really all about planning right and then making it happen. And, for the most part, the men are responsible for the good or bad outcome of the date. The question, then, is "What makes a good or bad date?"

Planning a Great Date

There are three keys that make a date great, and they form the acronym ME and U.

M: Memorable. Is the activity something that you and your date will remember (for good reasons)? Is it something that you both will especially enjoy?

E: Engaging. Is the activity something that will help you connect with your date? Is it an activity that will help you get to know each other better? Is it an active activity that requires participation and communication?

and

U: Uplifting. Is the activity testimony-building? Is it an experience that will bring you both closer to the Savior?

After one of his first dates with his future wife, President David O. McKay wrote in his journal: "Took a ride over on South hills. Saw purple [mountains] at sunset. Very beautiful. . . . Went strolling with [Emma Ray]. Told each other secrets. A memorable night!" His sweetheart added: "Yes, and we held hands all the way home."[2]

One thing to keep in mind in planning a great date is that the best ones are typically not the most expensive ones. Contrary to what the world might try to convince you, you don't need to use up your life savings to make a date great. Relationship expert John Gray said, "The fastest way of finding a special partner or being found by someone is to create positive dating experiences."[3]

Sam F. says, "It's okay to plan a date that isn't at the nicest restaurant or the most expensive movie theater. A girl is generally just happy with being with a guy who cares about her and who is honestly interested in helping her to a have great time."

We've included a list of suggested dating activities, along with their associated costs, that may be helpful in sparking some ideas. Dating creatively simply means planning an activity that is fun, wholesome, and that will be memorable (in a good way).

Activity	Cost
Aerobics class	$10
Ballroom dancing	$15
Basketball	free
BBQ	$10
Bike ride	free
Black-and-White movie	$5
Board games	free
Bonfire	$10
Bowling	$10
Build-your-own indoor golf course	$5
Candlelight dinner	$20
Canning	free
Canoeing	$25
Capture the flag	free
Card games	free
Card making	free
Charades	free
Chocolate making/dipping	$10
Clean a park	free
Clean someone's home	free
Cook a meal for the needy	$10
Cooking	$10
Crepe breakfast social	$10
Crime prevention class	$10
Dance	free
Dessert contest	$10
Dog walking	free
Drawing class	$10
Dutch oven cooking	$10
Etiquette/formal dining	$20
Family history	free
Family Home Evening	free
Fireside	free
Food storage	free
Games	free
Hike	free

History tour	$50
Ice skating	$15
Journal writing	free
Make Christmas gifts for children	free
Make a home movie	free
Martial Arts Class	$10
Paintball	$50
Painting	free
Petting zoo	$20
Photography	free
Picnic	$10
Pizza making	$10
Poetry readings	free
Potluck	$10
Pottery	$15
Racquetball	free
Read marriage articles	free
Rock climbing	$10
Scripture study	free
Sculpting class	$10
Service scavenger hunt	free
Singing in elderly homes	free
Storytelling to children	free
Swimming	free
Teach illiterate to read	free
Tennis	free
Theater	$20
Theme park	$50
Theme parties	$20
Treasure hunt	$15
Trunk or treat	$5
Tutor a child	free
Visit a museum	$10
Visit the elderly	free
Visit people in the hospital	free
Watch sunrise	free
Write letters to missionaries	free

Once you have decided on the activity, ensure that you have answered the other key questions that make for planning a great date.

Who? Who will you be going out with? How well do you know that person?

- Make sure to build at least a minimal relationship with the person you want to date. It's very important to build some rapport to begin with.
- When you call or talk to that person, think and talk about her or his interests more than your own, and really listen.

What? What will you do? Will you do multiple activities, like go to dinner with a group, and then go bowling as a couple? How fun will it be? Are you ensuring that it will be a morally uplifting experience?

- Consider doing a "hybrid" date: first go with a group to eat dinner, play capture the flag, or some other activity, and then separate into couples and go somewhere else. That way, you can see that person as they relate to a group of people, as well as encounter them in a one-on-one setting.
- Ensure that the activity is exciting for you as well. Being bored on a date is never attractive.

When? When will you go out? How far in advance will you invite the person?

- Call or talk to the person well in advance of the scheduled date. That way you have time to ask someone else out if that person can't go, and you have more time to make preparations for the date.
- Going out on the weekend, Friday or Saturday night is most common. But you can also schedule dates during the week. It's really up to you and the other person. Dating at night is the most common, but you can also go to lunch together, or play tennis, go shopping together, and so on. Be open minded about when you can go out, and you'll create more time to date in your busy schedule.

Where? Where will you go out? Are you planning to be in public places? If your date is somewhere remote, will you stay with a group of

CHRIS & JULIA DEAVER AND DON McCARTNEY

people so as to avoid morally questionable situations?

- Go to places that are beautiful, clean, and respectable. It helps the dating process.
- Don't ever sit in a parked car or in other dark places alone for very long. It can lead to serious sin. When the Spirit tells you to go elsewhere, don't ask questions. Just go.

Why? Is this someone you can see, at least for now, getting to know better and perhaps dating long-term? Is this someone you are genuinely interested in?

- Be careful of who you date and why you date this person. It is important to keep in mind the purpose of dating.

How? How are you going to prepare for the date? Have you made reservations for the dinner, bought tickets for the play, or otherwise effectively prepared?

- Write down a checklist of everything that needs to be done for the date and go through it well in advance and you won't have to worry about it later.

What's next? Is there anything else you can think of that needs to happen to make this date a success? Do it!

Remember, dating creatively before marriage is just as important as it is during marriage. In other words, the quest to demonstrate genuine love and affection is never over!

If dating is indeed the path to marriage, how exactly do you find the right person to be with for eternity through dating? Author John Gray said, "Finding the right person for you is like hitting the center of a target in archery. To aim and hit the center takes a lot of practice. Some people may hit the center right away, but most do not. In a similar way, most people date several people before finding the right one. Some people take much longer than necessary because something is missing in their approach. By exploring this metaphor from archery, we can clearly see what we may be lacking."[4]

Encourage the Date

So what can you do if you are a woman, and it is not your explicit responsibility (like it is for men) to ask out others on dates? Encourage guys to take the initiative. Make yourself attractive and available. Too many girls group themselves within a "force field" that inadvertently repels all males and makes potential social situations extremely awkward. Have you ever tried to ask someone out in front of a group of five other friends? It's not only intimidating, but for many guys, it's impossible. In other words, don't expect Prince Charming to break through a bunch of social obstacles you set in his path. If you do, you are only setting him up for failure and yourself up for disappointment. Instead, be friendly and social. Try to position yourself close to the guys you are most interested in. Millions of successfully married, righteous women testify that it works!

Sisters, regardless of whether you are getting asked out, you can make yourself attractive. You can start right now by creating the right circumstances for something great to happen. For example, Jane was looking for years for the right guy. Her biggest problem was a familiar one: she never got asked out! Jane's first response was to get upset and blame guys for being irresponsible and lazy. "After all, if guys were doing their job," Jane reasoned, "I would be married by now." In an effort to find answers, Jane wisely sought counsel from her bishop, who was a spiritual man. Jane asked her bishop why guys were so clueless. Her bishop asked what she was referring to specifically. Jane explained that she was not getting asked out at all.

After discussing her frustrations with her bishop, Jane looked him in the eyes and said, "I think I'm ready to call it quits and just sign on the dotted line to become a ministering angel." Jane's bishop quickly snapped back with the question, "What are you doing to make guys want to ask you out?"

Jane thought for several seconds and then responded, "I'm doing everything I can." Her bishop explained in detail how Jane could focus on herself, develop her talents, increase her education, continue to make herself attractive, and create opportunities for dating. He talked to her about finding opportunities to socialize in places like institute, stake dances, and other types of activities. He told her how important it was to focus on getting to know young men and that she ought to let herself shine and radiate in conversations with them. He promised her that if she did those things, she would be blessed with more opportunities.

Jane was somewhat skeptical but believed that her bishop was inspired. So, she followed his counsel by putting his recommendations into practice. So what happened? Jane didn't get a date every day, or even every week. But she had far more opportunities as she was asked out more by guys, and she enjoyed the dates greatly. Quality young men noticed her more as Jane radiated confidence and joy in her life, instead of worry and sadness at not getting asked out. Instead of feeling like a social leper, Jane felt like a lioness ready to face the future bravely.

Rachel B. offers this advice to other young women, "You need to find things you have in common. Make it easy for him to ask you out. Sometimes girls think guys should do all the work and they're supposed to sit back and relax. And that just isn't the case. Both people need to work at it."

Kim P. adds, "But a guy has to be the main pursuer in order to set in his own mind that she's worth going for. If a girl asks a guy out, then the guy still has to do the pursuing in subsequent dates or [be] more assertive in developing the relationship. Even if she initiated at the beginning, she still has to let him be in charge of how the relationship is going to go."

Jenna K. mentions, "Ladies, remember that dating is always your responsibility, too. No one can find a bunch of dates for you. You can't get mad at other people because they have more dates than you do. It's not easy for anybody. Everyone has to go through some pain whether it's before or after they're married."

Michelle O. says, "I think where I'm most assertive is in situations where I'm not sure if the guy likes me or he seems really shy. So I won't directly ask him out on a date, but I'll tell him something to the effect that there is a group of us going out to do something and invite him along, just to let him know that I am interested in getting to know him better. Then he can take it from that point on if he is interested in me."

 Only the flexibly creative person can really manage the future. Only the one who can face novelty with confidence and without fear.—Abraham Maslow

Set the Best Priorities

There are so many ways to spend your time that it's easy to get caught up in good but not essential activities. In a world filled with so many choices, how do you decide how to spend time in the best way? Some people wait in their apartments until someone invites them to do something. That may work if you have friends who are inclusive and proactive, but most often, depending solely on others is often a recipe for dating doom. After conducting interviews and research, we found that the greatest daters are also the greatest planners. They don't necessarily plan out every minute of every day, but they focus exclusively on what matters, and they make plans to achieve great things.

 Most people feel best about their work when they've cleaned up, closed up, clarified, and renegotiated all their agreements with themselves and others. Do this weekly instead of yearly.
—David Allen

Set aside time for one hour each weekend, on a Saturday or Sunday, to plan your week. Ponder on the following "Seven P's of Planning":

Purpose

Effective planning begins with a clear *purpose*. Purpose is the reason for the mission to be accomplished. For Jesus Christ, it is to "bring to pass the immortality and eternal life of man" (Moses 1:39). For you, it is to do all that you can to strive for eternal life.

Principles

Once you have established your *purpose*, the great big "why" behind what you do, move forward by deciding what *principles* will help you achieve your purpose—or the big "how." Principles are eternal truths like "love one another" that create long-term results. These truths don't ever disappear or diminish in power. Principles, when applied correctly, will lead you to consistent success.

Priorities

Let your *principles* determine your *priorities*. Priorities are specific areas to which you give time, whether you realize it or not. One priority would be that of loving your family, based on the principle of loving one another.

When you set priorities, you need to determine what activities will help you spend time making progress according to your purpose and principles. Ask yourself, "How does my time watching television rate compared to my time spent doing service?" Or, "Should I focus more on serving my family or earning money?" You can also use the following two questions as a basic gauge to prioritize your activities, "Does this activity help me grow physically, spiritually, emotionally, mentally, or otherwise? Is it helping to build someone else in any of these ways?" If not, think twice about that activity—it might be fun, but it's probably not that important.

Personas

Once you have set your course, based on godly *principles* and *priorities*, your work is only partly finished. Next, you must realize what *personas*, or roles, the Lord expects you to fulfill. Jesus Christ has had many roles and responsibilities with regard to Heavenly Father's children. He continues to be our Savior, Redeemer, Exemplar, and Advocate.

The Savior is the Son of God, son of earthly parents, brother, carpenter, friend, healer, and leader of the Church. During his mortal ministry, Jesus Christ was not imbalanced in His approach in fulfilling these roles. In fact, He was perfectly balanced in every endeavor. This meant that depending on the situation, he had to express softer or tougher love, teach essential doctrine, or heal someone. In other words, His life patterns flowed from His understanding of His particular roles. This takes not only great desire but also powerful confidence. You can know, like Jesus Christ knew, that Heavenly Father is there to back you up when you work for Him.

Plans

Plans ought to be based upon your *principles*, *priorities*, and *personas*. As you know, plans are specific instructions for achieving a goal. Write down SMART goals that are Specific, Measurable, Attainable, Realistic, and Time-based. Once you've listed your goals, break them down into smaller steps, then attack them with everything you've got.

Performance

You will achieve high *performance* as you work hard at your *principle*- and *purpose*-based *plans*. As you do, performing your best will become a powerful, unchanging pattern.

Patterns

Patterns, in the godliest sense of the word, are those habits you have established in your life that lead to solid, positive results. Daily scripture study and prayer are perfect examples. Additionally, a weekly service project is a rewarding pattern. Set Christlike patterns in your life, and they will become part of your permanent character. Powerful missionaries develop immovable, godly habits.

Measuring Success

Measure your performance as you move through this process of establishing your personal *purpose, principles, priorities, personas, plans, performances*, and *patterns*. Make note of the positive results you achieve and the areas in which you can improve. Focus positively on your goals. Envision successes before they happen. Look at your goals every day. Draw pictures or get photos of your goals as realities, hang them up, and look at them daily. Write objectives in your journal or write them on sticky pads and put them up everywhere to remember. Elder M. Russell Ballard said:

> I believe you can train yourself to become a positive thinker, but you must cultivate a desire to develop the skill of setting personal worthy and realistic goals. . . . I am so thoroughly convinced that if we don't set goals in our life and learn how to master the technique of living to reach our goals, we can reach a ripe old age and look back on our life only to see that we reached but a small part of our full potential. When one learns to master the principle of setting a goal, he will then be able to make a great difference in the results he attain in this life. . . .
>
> I would suggest that if you want to have success in the goal setting process, you learn to write your goals down. I would even put them in a very prominent place—on your mirror or on the refrigerator door. Keep your goals in front of you, in writing. Then, with the desire to reach your written goals, you will be more willing to pay the price that successful goal-oriented people must pay.[5]

One exercise that helps to measure and increase performance is to keep a "Power Journal" wherein you record all the great things you are accomplishing with the help of the Lord. This helps you build confidence and power to continue the achievement cycle. Measure your daily performance against your goal to see how you're progressing.

In setting goals, be specific and write down measurable and attainable goals. Then break each goal down into bite-size, weekly goals. Be sure to avoid vague goals like, "I will have charity." A goal like that has no when or how. A better goal is " I will pray sincerely for charity two times each day."

As the author of your own love story, always consider how your attitude and actions ensure that you are seeking the help of the Lord by adjusting your will to His. In your weekly preparation for the upcoming days, ponder and focus on what is most important to you. Make prayer a part of all of your planning efforts. The Lord gives the following counsel:

> For behold, it is not meet that I should command in all things; for he that is compelled in all things, the same is a slothful and not a wise servant; wherefore he receiveth no reward.
>
> Verily I say, men should be anxiously engaged in a good cause, and do many things of their own free will, and bring to pass much righteousness;
>
> For the power is in them, wherein they are agents unto themselves. And inasmuch as men do good they shall in nowise lose their reward. (D&C 58:26–28)

Build a Friendship

Elder Spencer W. Kimball wrote: "The successful marriage depends in large measure upon the preparation made in approaching it. . . . One cannot pick the ripe, rich, luscious fruit from a tree that was never planted, nurtured, nor pruned."[6]

Building a friendship requires creating trust. Trust is built as you say nice things to people, but validation comes through taking action and actually showing people that you mean what you say. The more you are able to emit caring and compassion, the more you will be able to build trust. Another step in gaining the trust of others is to see the world from their perspective. As you do this, your understanding of the challenges, obstacles, and triumphs that you experience will be greatly enriched. This is achieved through sincere communication, especially through empathic listening.

Not only is it important for us to be able to gain others' trust, it is equally important for us to trust those whom we are dating. One basic way to show that we trust them is by truly being ourselves when we're with them. When we share our thoughts, feelings, perspectives, and beliefs we are demonstrating to those we date that we trust them.

The most important thing we can do to build trust in others is to trust in the individual plan that the Lord has for each of us. Sometimes it gets very difficult to understand why things either are or aren't happening. You may wonder why you aren't married yet when it feels like you are doing everything possible to facilitate this process, and especially when it seems like all your friends and associates have "settled down." It helps to remember that the Lord has different timetables for each of us. The underlying principle here is that it doesn't matter how old we are when we get married. What matters is that we remain true and faithful to the Lord and to the covenants which we have made, while striving to do everything we can to qualify for His promised blessings.

When we develop trust and faith in the Lord, we will have a foundation in our lives that will not fail. We will be able to rely on him when we face dating and other challenges. He will be there for us. When we have triumphs and moments of glory in life, the Lord will sweeten these moments. We will be able to discern the plan the Lord has for us in mortality and the great blessings that await us in the eternities to come.

It's much more effective to build a friendship before getting married and not the other way around. Eric and Sarah met each other while attending the same ward and spent time together informally, at first. Eric visited Sarah in her apartment and got to know her roommates. He became friends with Sarah, learned her likes and dislikes, and got a good idea of what her dreams were. Then, Eric asked Sarah on a date to dinner and miniature golf. They had a great time and got to know each other even better. After several months of dating, Eric and Sarah realized that they had become best friends, so making the decision to get married wasn't difficult. Great friendships make for great marriages.

Create Happiness

Everyone wants to be happy, but happiness does not come easily, particularly in dating. However, when you are striving to do what is right, you are on the path of happiness. That path is one that many throughout history have walked, including such great people as Lehi and Sariah, Jacob and Rachel, and Abraham and Sarah.

Happiness and repentance are very good friends. In fact, they are always together. The more you truly repent, the happier you are. True repentance requires confessing and forsaking sins completely. It requires a change of heart. When you approach the Lord in total honesty and repent of your sins, you gain access to a peace that only repentance can bring, which is the secret to happiness. King Benjamin described it this way:

> And again, believe that ye must repent of your sins and forsake them, and humble yourselves before God; and ask in sincerity of heart that he would forgive you; and now, if you believe all these things see that ye do them.
>
> And again I say unto you as I have said before, that as ye have come to the knowledge of the glory of God, or if ye have known of his goodness and have tasted of his love, and have received a remission of your sins, which causeth such exceedingly great joy in your souls, even so I would that ye should remember, and always retain in remembrance, the greatness of God, and your own nothingness, and his goodness and long-suffering towards you, unworthy creatures, and humble yourselves even in the depths of humility, calling on the name of the Lord daily, and standing steadfastly in the faith of that which is to come, which was spoken by the mouth of the angel.
>
> And behold, I say unto you that if ye do this ye shall always rejoice, and be filled with the love of God, and always retain a remission of your sins; and ye shall grow in the knowledge of the glory of him that created you, or in the knowledge of that which is just and true. (Mosiah 4:10–12)

Be Bold

To date fearlessly means to act with boldness, to take chances, and to be spontaneous. Alma told his son Shiblon that he should "use boldness, but not overbearance" (Alma 38:12). Those who demonstrate overbearance are easy to identify as the annoying guys or girls who never seem to get a clue but always do way too much to be noticed. On the other hand, those who are bold can be recognized fairly easily as those who do not shrink from challenging circumstances, but willingly move forward even when things may be unclear or seem risky.

 Have faith in your abilities! Without a humble but reasonable confidence in your own powers you cannot be successful or happy. —Norman Vincent Peale

Joseph had tried many different methods to find Sister Right, but to no avail. But he kept trying, and he was bold. After awhile, he felt stuck. He moved to Utah in an effort to continue his search in a place with a high concentration of LDS girls. One day, Joseph was shopping for groceries when he noticed a beautiful girl in one of the lines. He stepped immediately into line behind her. He said hello, and then they exchanged some basic information, like their names, where they were from, and so on. He noticed that she was holding a grocery list and asked, "Can I see your list for a second?" She handed it to him, and he noticed it had items with check marks next to them. He wrote. "Email Joseph," and wrote down his email address. He handed her the list and said, "Looks like you missed one thing." She laughed.

Joseph walked away from that situation having been extremely bold, but not certain if she would contact him. Soon after, however, she sent him an email asking him to do something sometime. The result? They dated for several months, got engaged, and were married in the temple shortly thereafter. The key? Boldness.

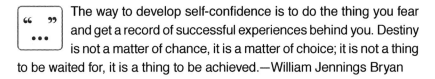

The way to develop self-confidence is to do the thing you fear and get a record of successful experiences behind you. Destiny is not a matter of chance, it is a matter of choice; it is not a thing to be waited for, it is a thing to be achieved.—William Jennings Bryan

....

1. Dallin H. Oaks, "Dating versus Hanging Out," *Ensign*, June 2006, 10–16.
2. David Laurence McKay, *My Father, David O. McKay* (Salt Lake City: Deseret Book, 1989), 2.
3. John Gray, *Mars and Venus on a Date: A Guide for Navigating the 5 States of Dating* (New York: Harper, 1999), 6.
4. Ibid, 9.
5. M. Russell Ballard, "Do Things That Make a Difference," *Ensign*, June 1983, 68.
6. Spencer W. Kimball, *The Miracle of Forgiveness* (Salt Lake City: Bookcraft, 1969), 242.

Week Five Commitment: *For men*—pick an activity, plan it, pay for it (if it's not free), and then pair off with someone you are interested in and have a great time. *For women*—go out of your way to facilitate a great date by making a conscious effort to introduce the topic casually in conversation with someone you like (for example: "Oh! You like bowling, too? We should play some time.")

My Planned Activity

_____

_____

_____

_____

_____

_____

_____

_____

_____

_____

6

Ponder Perfection

A Real Look at Your Top 10 List

The best way to avoid divorce from an unfaithful, abusive, or unsupportive spouse is to avoid marriage to such a person. If you wish to marry well, inquire well. Associations through "hanging out" or exchanging information on the Internet are not a sufficient basis for marriage. There should be dating, followed by careful and thoughtful and thorough courtship. There should be ample opportunities to experience the prospective spouse's behavior in a variety of circumstances. Fiancés should learn everything they can about the families with whom they will soon be joined in marriage. In all of this, we should realize that a good marriage does not require a perfect man or a perfect woman. It only requires a man and a woman committed to strive together toward perfection.—Elder Dallin H. Oaks[1]

In a world where "perfect" so often is understood as flawlessly attractive, rich, or famous, it may be surprising to some people to realize that "perfect" actually means something entirely different to the Lord. One of the missions of the Church of Jesus Christ of Latter-day Saints is to "perfect the Saints." If you are striving to do all you can, you experience a certain level of perfection in the Lord Jesus Christ. That is, you rely on the Atonement of Jesus Christ and are able to lean on His perfection.

Christina M. says, "I don't want to be that person who is looking for somebody who is perfect and misses out on an opportunity to date somebody who is really great just because I am looking for perfection.

71

That totally perfect 'Hollywood' person doesn't really exist, anyway."

 We come to love not by finding a perfect person, but by learning to see an imperfect person perfectly.
—Anonymous

Obviously, no one but the Savior is sinless. Therefore, it would be delusional to look around for the perfect spouse (because if he was perfect he would already be translated and no longer available). The key is to look for the spouse who is in the business of perfecting himself with the Lord's help. In other words, he is striving to meet the Lord's expectations for his life and being the very best he can be. Yes, he may still have some faults and weaknesses, but he is striving to be worthy before the Lord.

Kevin H. says, "I'm looking for someone who will complement me. Where I lack, I want her to be strong and where she lacks, I want to be strong. I want someone who's motivated and goal-oriented, someone who can help me be the best person that I can be."

Now, let's bring this even closer to home. Finding the right spouse requires you to do two things: first, consider everything you hope your future spouse is looking for and striving to be; second, work to attract all of those things. It can be likened to applying for your ideal job. As you go through the application process, you take every step to learn all you can about the position. You find out about the hours, the job expectations, the people with whom you'll be working, and the company's history. You don't just look into things superficially, rather, you leave no stone unturned in your search about this position. You also measure and share with the interviewer exactly what you are willing to do to help make them successful. On the same note, the company is looking for someone qualified in a particular way, who fits its expectations. It's a shared process, but you definitely need to do your homework. Dating is no different.

 Do you love me because I am beautiful or am I beautiful because you love me?
—Oscar Hammerstein, *Cinderella*

When we interviewed Dale Murphy, former Atlanta Braves outfielder, two-time MVP, and former president of the Massachusetts Boston mission, about his dating experience, he said, "In 1978, I went to school at BYU and met my wife there. We had mutual friends. I just kind of knew she was the right one. You just know."[2]

Mike A. adds: "Light attracts light. You need to be a person with those qualities to attract someone with those qualities" (see D&C 88:40).

Trisha B. mentions, "I'm very much attracted to guys who can make others feel good around them no matter who they are around."

Aaron D. suggests, "Take out two or three different girls and then as you get more serious with one, you back off from the others. This gives you the opportunity to figure out what you're looking for."

Seek Spirituality

Being "in love" and attracted to a person is important, but definitely not enough. President Gordon B. Hinckley said, "Choose a companion of your own faith. You are much more likely to be happy. Choose a companion you can always honor, you can always respect, one who will complement you in your own life, one to whom you can give your entire heart, your entire love, your entire allegiance, your entire loyalty."[3]

When President Hinckley encouraged singles to "choose a companion of your own faith" he meant it in the general sense of choosing a member of the Church of Jesus Christ of Latter-day Saints as well as in the particular sense of choosing someone who is equally committed to the Lord. Being "equally yoked" with your spouse is an important key to success. Some people, for example, attend their Church meetings, but perhaps do not accept callings, hold family home evening weekly, pray regularly, or study their scriptures daily. If you are more oriented toward obedience in those areas, would you be happy with someone who was less so? If the companionship is to work out well, then the answer is most likely no. Consider such things as you approach this important decision of who to date and marry.

Elder Richard G. Scott has said the following: "As you seek an eternal companion, look for someone who is developing the essential attributes that bring happiness: a deep love of the Lord and of His commandments, a determination to live them, one that is kindly, understanding, forgiving of others, and willing to give of self, with the desire to have a family crowned with beautiful children and a commitment to teach them the principles of truth in the home."[4]

Remember, it is important that you pursue one who is interested in having a righteous family. This is a concept that has eternal implications. If you fail to get to know the person you are dating, you may find that your potential spouse may be someone who doesn't want to have kids. Cary was on a date with Craig. She was impressed with him—he seemed to be fairly involved in the ward and active in doing important things in his education and career. After she got in his car and they spent a few minutes conversing, Cary had a revelation. When she asked Craig about his future dreams, he did not include anything about having children. Cary pressed him on the issue, asking him if he looked forward to being a father at some point after marriage to the right person. Craig shocked her with his answer: "I've really got to just focus on my career and maybe finding the right person. I'd like to have a dog, but kids are not on my agenda in the future."

After hearing Craig share his thoughts on having children, Cary asked Craig if they could return to her house. Craig wasn't sure why they would do that, but he turned the car around and they went back. At that point, Cary stepped out of the car and thanked Craig for his time. Craig looked stunned and blurted, "But we didn't even get dinner! Or go bowling!"

Cary responded that based on what he'd said about his future goals, things would not work out between them. She expressed that it was one of her most important desires to have a family and that it was obvious that they didn't share that goal, and therefore they were not compatible. Craig was horribly disappointed, but Cary walked away happy, knowing that she was being selective about the right things. And Craig saved himself some time being with someone who was not compatible.

Sometimes people encourage singles to "not be so picky." This is good advice in the sense that you should have an open mind, but you should never compromise crucial values that you need to share with your spouse. Stop dating someone—even in the middle of the date—if they don't share your values. Walk out of a movie on a date if that movie doesn't adequately represent your values. Stop speaking with someone if she isn't positive or uplifting. Never date someone who has low standards.

As you get to know the people you date, you can get an understanding of their commitment to the gospel. There are many ways to measure this. One of the best ways is to notice how they spend their time. Are they active in their local ward? Do they fulfill their church responsibilities (home or visiting teaching, callings, and other assignments) faithfully? Do they attend the temple? How do they treat their roommates, friends, family members, and other associates?

Dane W. says, "I want someone who helps me by making me want to be better, not by putting their fist down and saying I need to be better. I want someone who motivates me because of the way she is and whom I motivate because of the way that I am. Then we can grow together."

Another consideration is their attitude in performing their duties. What is their attitude like? Why do they do what they do? The Lord has clearly said, "For behold, God hath said a man being evil cannot do that which is good; for if he offereth a gift, or prayeth unto God, except he shall do it with real intent it profiteth him nothing. For behold, it is not counted unto him for righteousness. For behold, if a man being evil giveth a gift, he doeth it grudgingly; wherefore it is counted unto him the same as if he had retained the gift; wherefore he is counted evil before God" (Moroni 7:6–8).

When we internalize the message of the gospel of Jesus Christ, we will have softer hearts and more appreciation for the opportunity to render service to others. We will be able to distance ourselves from having a "what's in it for me" attitude while helping others out.

We display our love for the Lord by setting an example through our actions. As you humbly seek to serve those around you, members of the opposite sex will take notice, and they'll come to know of your true testimony and convictions about the gospel.

Jeff is one of the best examples of someone who quietly went about providing service to others. His personality was not gregarious, yet he had a powerful testimony of the gospel of Jesus Christ and what it had done for him, and he shared it often with others. His greatness lay in his consistency. Besides being one of the most knowledgeable people about the scriptures, Jeff always attended his Church meetings, was a great home teacher and friend, and was worthy to give blessings whenever requested. Jeff's love for his fellow men was enormous and shone in his example.

Some people do all they can in Church, but portray "holier than thou" attitudes. This mind-set often manifests itself through criticizing or gossiping about others' perceived faults and shortcomings. The old adage that talk is cheap really is true. In the scriptures we read, "Wherefore, by their fruits ye shall know them" (Matthew 7:20). Proving your beliefs by acting on them is essential to successful discipleship. And acting on your beliefs means relying on the power of Jesus Christ and His perfection. Author Stephen E. Robinson said:

> Yes, we are very good at telling each other and ourselves how perfect we must be to inherit the kingdom. It's just that too often we forget to tell each other how this perfection is to be gained. You see, there is a trick to it—a shortcut. And if you don't know the trick, the shortcut to perfection, you can burn yourself out trying to become perfect on your own. The great secret is this: Jesus Christ will share his perfection, his sinlessness, his righteousness, his merits with us. In his mercy he offers us the use of his perfection, in the absence of our own, to satisfy the demands of justice. [5]

 I love you, not only for what you are, but for what I am when I am with you.—Roy Croft

Consider Heritage

Family heritage plays an important role as you consider selecting your spouse. Get to know your future spouse's parents, brothers, and sisters. Doing so will help you gather a more complete picture of who your potential spouse is and who she is likely to become. One oft-repeated counsel is that if you want to know what a guy will be like in the future, just look at his dad. Likewise, if you want to know what a girl will be like in the future, just look at her mom. Certainly it is true that parents wield a powerful influence in the upbringing of children.

As you look forward to new and continued dating adventures, keep in mind the influence of family on both you and the person you date. President David O. McKay taught, "In choosing a companion, it is necessary to study the disposition, the inheritance, and training of the one with whom you are contemplating making life's journey."[6]

It is, however, truly a blessing that we know that our backgrounds do not have to dictate the outcome of our lives. While we can do little to change our DNA, we *can* choose how we respond to the events and conditions of our upbringing, and while we're dating is one of the most opportune times to do so.

Your greatest tool to help create your future—regardless of the circumstances in which you were raised—is a thorough study the Book of Mormon. In the Book of Mormon, many individuals overcame the false traditions of their fathers. Likewise, there were many who adopted the correct traditions of their fathers and followed them in righteousness. When the Lamanite people converted to the gospel of Jesus Christ and became the Anti-Nephi-Lehies, they buried their weapons of war and promised to never go to war again. Their children, however, known as Helaman's stripling warriors, had also converted to the gospel of Jesus Christ and committed to defend their families, land, and religion with the sword.

In your life, you will need to commit, like the fathers of the stripling warriors, to never do certain things that are wrong, regardless what you may have been taught. This may mean eliminating such behaviors as being quick to anger, being addicted to spending, or being apathetic to the needs of others. Like the stripling warriors themselves, you will also need to commit to always do certain things that are right. This may mean adopting behaviors like being patient and tolerant, standing up for righteousness no matter the cost, and sharing the gospel when you know you should.

Remember Respect

 That you may retain your self-respect, it is better to displease the people by doing what you know is right, than to temporarily please them by doing what you know is wrong.
—William J. H. Boetcker

Jana G. says, "I believe respect is one of the most important things in a relationship of trying to get to know each other and also just building relationships."

Respect is the key to solving many of the challenges in a developing relationship. Respect is important in two forms: respect for yourself and respect for your date. A guy shows respect for himself by not asking a girl out repeatedly if she is always rejecting him. Guys need to find a good balance between being persistent and determining when to move on. The number of times and amount of patience a guy has with any one girl can vary. Some guys have followed the "three strikes" rule—give a girl three chances to accept an invitation to go out on a date and then move on.

In dating, respect is reflected in many ways. Sometimes, individuals date people who do not reciprocate the respect that they themselves are willing to show. For example, James had been dating a girl for quite a while and was always the one calling her. One day, James was ecstatic when she called him—for the first time in six months! Apparently, James possessed a high tolerance for doing all the work in their relationship. Most people, however, would not be interested in such a relationship, as it illustrates a situation where the parties are not evenly sharing respect.

Guys need to recognize that if the girl says she's unavailable for a date, her reason often matters. Does the girl seem genuine in her response, such as "I have a big test the day of the date" or "my cousin's getting married"? Or does she give the old "I need to wash my hair" excuse?

Brandon L. says, "The best dates I have had are when I go out with someone and we're both self-respecting people and we both respect each other."

Remember that there are a lot of people out there that you could potentially marry. One problem is that single people sometimes get stuck in the rut of lingering on their last (or first) love. It's okay to be sad for a day or two about an ended relationship, but spending months and months dwelling on it will only put you in a mental trap. By staying focused on your last girlfriend or boyfriend, you can't spend the time and energy needed trying to find your true, eternal love! Don't get stuck in the past. Focus on the present and future.

Ladies can show that they have self-respect by not being too intense in pursuing a guy, especially at the start of a relationship. This is not to say that girls shouldn't be proactive, but there is a major difference between girls who are proactive and those who are domineering. For example, proactive girls give guys sincere compliments when they are on a date or in a situation when they are getting to know a guy. Proactive girls make an effort to befriend and talk to a guy they are potentially interested in. Domineering girls, on the other hand, continually force themselves on the object of their affection, much to the chagrin of the guy.

Even we, the authors, know about these types of frustrations. Don went through a similar experience:

> During my college years, I had a roommate whom many females found physically attractive. I remember it was springtime, and we had just moved to a new building complex and into a new ward.

There was a girl who spoke with my roommate once at a social gathering and instantly became infatuated with him. She would call him multiple times in one week, and worse yet, many times she would show up at our apartment during the week, often unannounced. I say that it was worse when she came over, because a lot of the time we would be watching basketball or hanging out, and it always made my roommate feel like he had to entertain her. All this action on her part would have been warranted had my roommate been reciprocating and calling her or going over to her place, but he wasn't. For a time it didn't seem like she picked up his clues of not being interested, but finally after a while, she relented.

One way for girls to show guys that they respect them is to return their phone calls. If you are a girl who is simply not interested in a guy, you should just tell him—politely, but directly. His feelings may be hurt momentarily, but he will recover. If you don't clearly let him know that you are not interested, you run the risk of having a permanent affection-seeker hunting you down. You owe it to the guy to let him know you are, in fact, not interested.

Guys can show respect by asking girls out in a respectful, comfortable way. A guy should get to know a girl—at least a little bit, by having a few conversations with her—before asking her out. Any guy who has flipped through the phone book and dialed random numbers to ask out girls knows such a practice is ineffective. Even guys who are risk-taking, yet effective daters know that girls like to exchange information and feel comfortable around a guy before spending a few hours over dinner and miniature golf.

Guys can show respect toward their dates by exercising timeliness. We have all heard the expression that "time is money." Time is actually more than money—it is a valuable resource that disappears quickly. You may be able to find the lost dollar bill from three weeks ago, but you will never have another May 19, 2010 during your time here on earth. If a girl has committed herself to spending an evening with you, the least you can do for her is show up at her place on time. There may be times when you are running behind, or something may come up that prevents you from being punctual, and that's what a phone is for. Practicing timeliness goes for girls too. You are not showing great respect when the guy shows up and you make him wait fifteen or twenty minutes while you put finishing touches on your makeup, or if you aren't home when he comes to pick you up.

Don states,

Mandy lived in the building complex next to mine. During the summer, one of my friends from work lived in her complex and I met her at one of the ward activities that I attended with him. During the weeks leading up to school, I had swung by and visited with her at her apartment three times. While I was visiting with her, she was always attentive and seemed genuinely interested in getting to know me better. Between the times that I visited her, I ran into her while she was getting her mail. At the time she was on the phone, but she acted friendly toward me and even told me to come by again and visit her.

After this incident and the other times that I had spent at visiting with her, I decided that a date was warranted. So I fired away and set up a lunch date for us one Saturday afternoon. When I arrived at her place to pick her up, however, she wasn't there! In fact, no one was there! I tried to remain calm and retreated to my apartment, deciding that I would come back in fifteen minutes to give it one final try. As I took in some college football with my roommates, my mind started racing, and all I kept thinking was, "I can't believe this is happening to me!"

Finally after what seemed like an eternity, the fifteen minutes had expired and I trudged my way back to her place. Though Mandy still wasn't home, her roommate was. When her roommate came to the door and saw me standing there she said, "Oh weren't you suppose to have a date with Mandy today?"

"That's what I thought also," I said.

Her roommate, recognizing the awkwardness of the moment, instantly invited me in. She then tried to call Mandy on her cell phone, but to no avail. So, for a good fifteen or twenty minutes, the roommate and I just made small talk, and I could tell things were hitting rock bottom in our conversation when she started asking me what my favorite color was. I was about ready to call it quits on my supposed date with Mandy as it was approaching 12:40 p.m. and we had set noon as our original date time when the phone unexpectedly rang. It was Mandy, who was apologizing profusely and explaining how she had got stuck waiting at the car wash. She told me she would be home soon and then we could go to lunch. Needless to say, it was an extremely frustrating experience."

Focus on the Right One

During their courtship, President Ezra Taft Benson and his wife "talked for hours, exploring their feelings about a future together. . . . The more they talked, the more comfortable they felt with each other." The prophet himself describes it this way: "'There was so much to tell and we seemed to enjoy each other so very much. . . . It was a perfect courtship during which I discovered in Flora a great character and a rare combination of virtues'"[6]

No matter how many dates you have or haven't been on, no matter how many good people you have met, some of the greatest moments of your dating life are yet to be lived. Shouldn't they be spent with someone you look forward to being with? This issue of respect that we have been discussing breaks right down to the issue of who you are and who you hope to date and marry. Below is a short list of attributes for the best and worst types of guys and girls. Study it and you'll find that the best people to meet are likely the type of person you want to become. Keep this list for the future as a tool for making the right decisions in dating, like never going out with a Wrong One. While no one is likely to possess all of the characteristics listed, a person may demonstrate several, which—depending on which side of the chart you're reading—is either cause for concern or rejoicing.

The "Right One"

- Prays regularly
- Reads the scriptures daily
- Attends the temple often
- Exercises regularly
- Actively pursues more education
- Accepts and magnifies any and all callings or assignments
- Works hard at work and sets long-term career goals
- Enjoys participating in ward activities and meeting new people
- Watches only entertainment that invites the Spirit and is uplifting
- Listens with empathy in conversations
- Respects parents and authorities
- Has specific, worthy goals in life
- Has self-discipline with regard to anger and bad language
- Knows how to save money and stay out of debt

- Shares thoughtful responses and is complimentary of others
- Wants to raise children to the Lord
- Works hard to be attractive and puts a lot of thought into dressing stylishly and modestly
- Is kind and very "us"-oriented
- Shares the gospel with everyone
- Sets a good example

The "Wrong One"

- Prays when all else fails
- Reads scriptures if it's convenient
- Attends the temple infrequently
- Considers walking from the TV to the refrigerator "an intense workout"
- Generally avoids educational opportunities
- Avoids the bishop on Sundays so as to not "worry about getting a calling"
- Does the bare minimum to pay the cable bill
- Would rather stay at home alone playing video games
- Watches anything, regardless of its effect on his or her spirituality.
- Participates in conversations only to be heard
- Disrespects parents and authorities
- Does not have specific goals in life
- Uses bad language often, and gets angry easily.
- Never saves money—that's what credit cards are for.
- Will say anything to get a laugh, even if it is offensive to others
- Thinks kids are more trouble than they're worth.
- Gives little thought to appearances and would rather be comfortable than attractive
- Is rude and very "me"-oriented
- Doesn't share the gospel at all
- Sets a bad example

Stay Focused on What Matters

Remember that dating for a great marriage is more than opening your heart to any girl with a pretty face or any boy that asks you out. Be picky.

Don't put your heart on the line for just anyone. Sisters, that young man who has the wonderful opportunity to spend precious hours with you is truly blessed. And yes, you will be gracing him with your presence. Just like the Lord sifts the wheat from the tares, you will need to be selective. Sift the guys best suited for you from those who are not. This includes determining who is truly interested in you and who is not.

We would all agree that important purchases, like which car to choose or what house to buy, should take a great amount of consideration. Even more so, the choice of whom to date seriously requires the best thinking and praying possible. You'll need to look at things from multiple angles and consider what a future would be like with any given individual, but you should also allow for some flexibility. You will not be flexible on standards, of course (would you buy a car with shoddy breaks?), but you shouldn't allow less important matters be deal breakers (you can survive without the killer sound system, if the car is safe and sensible). One young man met the girl of his dreams. He thought she was beautiful, spiritually mature, excited to have a family, and she seemed to be very interested in him. He only had one problem with her—she didn't know how to dance! So what did he do? He discarded that item from his list and pursued her anyway. What happened? They are now happily married with several children, he is now serving as the bishop of his ward, and most important, he is still absolutely in love with his wife. Flexibility in trivial things is appropriate for finding the right person.

• •

1. Dallin H. Oaks, "Divorce," *Ensign,* May 2007, 70–73.
2. Dale Murphy, interviewed by the authors.
3. Gordon B. Hinckley, "Life's Obligations," *Ensign*, Feb. 1999, 2.
4. Richard G. Scott, "Receive the Temple Blessings," *Ensign*, May 1999, 26.
5. Steven E. Robinson, *Believing Christ* (Salt Lake City: Deseret Book, 1992), 14.
6. David O. McKay, *Gospel Ideals* (Salt Lake City: Deseret Book, 1953), 459.

Week Six Commitment: Write down the top ten things you want in your spouse, and then look at them realistically. Decide which of those qualities really matter to your eternal happiness and which ones don't. Circle the items that matter, and cross out the ones that don't. Keep this list and refer to it regularly. Be willing to add and remove things on the list.

Top Ten Things I Want in My Spouse

1. _____

_____

2. _____

_____

3. _____

_____

4. _____

_____

5. _____

_____

6. _____

_____

7. _____

_____

8. _____

_____

9. _____

_____

10. _____

_____

7

Keep the Commandments

Staying Pure in an Impure World

[We] are faced constantly with modern-day Goliaths in the form of temptations that would cause us to violate our covenants and the standards the Lord has given us. This becomes even more important when you are surrounded daily with profanity, socially accepted immorality, immodesty, pornography, and other inappropriate material in the media, including television and the Internet, and widespread availability of drugs and alcohol. In a word, not a day goes by that we are not asked, in one form or another, "Who's on the Lord's side? Who?"—Elder Charles W. Dahlquist II [1]

Chris learned the importance of making good choices at an early age:

When I was eight years old, I looked forward to the release of a video game called *Double Dragon*. I read about it in magazines and learned everything I could so I would be prepared for the time when I could play it on my prized Nintendo 8-bit system. I was so eager; I told everyone about it. But I also knew I would have to save up several weeks of allowance to ever afford it—so it would be a long time before I could ever have the game.

At school one day, a boy named Brian—also a member of the Church—told me that he had *Double Dragon* at his house and invited me to come and play it. I almost jumped right out of my little chair! And you surely would have felt like I did, knowing that you would soon be experiencing the ultimate special effects in NES gaming!

After getting mother's approval, I went to Brian's house the next day to play. As soon as I got there, I scoured the house with my eyes, eager to see the coveted game. Brian waved it in front of me, and said, "You want to play *this*?" My heart pounded nervously as I defeated foes and progressed to the next level. Then, suddenly Brian jumped to his feet and told me to come outside. I reluctantly set the video game control on the floor and followed. We ran around playing tag for a while and then hide-and-go-seek. After trying to find Brian for a minute, I suddenly smelled something unfamiliar. It was smoke. Was something burning? I looked around and saw a cloud above a small, fenced area in the yard. I stepped into the fenced area and saw Brian puffing a cigarette. Brian waved it in front of me and smiled.

My thoughts were racing a hundred miles an hour. Wasn't Brian a member of the Church? Didn't he care about being good? Brian stared at me, tried to hand me a cigarette, and said, "Here. Smoke this. . . . it's fun." I looked at the cigarette without touching it and said no. Then, Brian offered something that I did not expect. He said, "If you smoke just one of these, I'll give you that *Double Dragon* game." It was, by far, the greatest temptation I had ever faced. I thought about how badly I wanted that video game, how long I would otherwise have to wait to buy it, and how much it would mean to me to have it. And then I thought about the cigarette and what it meant to smoke it, and that I had made a promise to the Savior never to smoke.

After what seemed like an eternity, I got courageous and said, "No. I won't do it for anything." Brian was stunned. He repeated his offer, but to no avail. I walked away. As I sat down on the sidewalk, thinking the situation through, I realized that I was sad I couldn't have *Double Dragon* right then. Those graphics and interactive capabilities were truly amazing. But I knew I had made the right choice.

As I look back now, I am always thankful I made the right choice that day. Not only did I avoid temptation, but I put off momentary pleasure for something greater—the peace of mind of living God's commandments. In the end, several weeks after that episode, I traded Brian for the *Double Dragon* video game with a game that I didn't care for. So, in the long run, I actually got what I wanted and kept my soul intact. In dating and marriage, it is no different. You can stay pure by avoiding evil situations and then experience the power that integrity brings, especially later, as you are married.

Choose the Right *Now*

No wonder Alma counseled his son, "And also see that ye bridle all your passions, that ye may be filled with love" (Alma 38:12). This scripture indicates that you must "bridle" your passions, or postpone them for later, when the time is right, after marriage. It also indicates that purity prepares you for charity. In other words, chastity and charity are intertwined. Being chaste literally prepares your soul to possess the greatest gift of all: charity. Author Dawn Eden expressed:

> Today, as the baby boomers begin collecting Social Security, the once-rebellious ideal of free love has become as American as Cherry Garcia ice cream. In an age where sexual mores are set by the likes of Britney, Lindsay, Paris, and their greatest inspiration, Carrie Bradshaw of "Sex and the City," the true rebels are those young adults who are striving to attain a love that goes beyond sex. Like their parents, they make a free choice—and their choice is to pursue that long-forgotten virtue known as chastity.[2]

Chastity is, in the words of Dr. Mark Lowery, associate professor of theology at the University of Dallas, "that virtue by which we are in control of our sexual appetite rather than it being in control of us."[3] Unlike mere abstinence, which is purely physical, *chastity* flowers from within. While part of it does mean having sex only within marriage, it is not just about sex, it's about love. Chastity is a lifelong journey of learning to love every individual in the fullest possible way—whether a friend, a relative, a spouse, or a stranger.

The Internet, television, movies, and many conversations throughout the world are loaded with explicit, titillating material designed to destroy souls. Satan seeks to make people miserable like himself—especially in dating. Satan will never be married and will never know joy, so he wants us to experience that same eternal doom and gloom. More than anything, he tries to destroy families. And he doesn't have to destroy families if he can prevent them from being created in the first place. His strategy is to tempt people to be immoral and disrupt their opportunities for marriage. Satan desperately wants to get good single people to think about sex constantly, and to kiss and touch inappropriately.

During the dating process, temptation will be present and it will be very powerful. You can't think that because you've served an honorable mission or were president of your Mia Maid class or teachers quorum that you are immune to the buffetings of Satan. Temptation will be present in your dating life. You have to respect that fact, but you cannot succumb to it. Like Joseph, who ran from Potiphar's wife and her seductions, you must avoid spiritually destructive situations that present themselves.

The Lord gave us sexual desire for a reason, and it is to be expressed only in marriage and only with that person with whom you have made covenants. The difference between expressing sexual feelings with someone even one day before getting married and waiting one day after is that to do the first is a destructive sin and to do the other is a holy blessing. It's that simple. Elder Jeffrey R. Holland expresses it this way:

> The body is an essential part of the soul. This distinctive and very important Latter-day Saint doctrine underscores why sexual sin is so serious. We declare that one who uses the God-given body of another without divine sanction abuses the very soul of that individual, abuses the central purpose and processes of life, "the very key" to life, as President Boyd K. Packer once called it. In exploiting the body of another—which means exploiting his or her soul—one desecrates the Atonement of Christ, which saved that soul and which makes possible the gift of eternal life. And when one mocks the Son of Righteousness, one steps into a realm of heat hotter and holier than the noonday sun. You cannot do so and not be burned.[3]

If this is the case, why would the Lord in His infinite wisdom give us this intense desire and power, expecting us to put off its use until later? Elder Holland further teaches that sexual intimacy is reserved for a married couple because it is the ultimate symbol of total union. Sex is not only a physical union between spouses but also a symbol of total union in all areas of their lives. In other words, sex was never intended for use outside of the bounds of marriage because it simply does not have use outside the bounds of marriage. That is, sexual indiscretions such as passionate kissing, pornography, masturbation, petting, fornication, and adultery all represent not only a violation in God's law but a violation in the principles of the reality of achieving happiness. The promised joy in marriage is only possible in obedience to God in these matters. Elder Jeffrey R. Holland states:

From the Garden of Eden onward, marriage was intended to mean the complete merger of a man and a woman—their hearts, hopes, lives, love, family, future, everything. This is a union of such completeness that we use the word *seal* to convey its eternal promise. But such a total union between a man and a woman can only come with the permanence afforded in a marriage covenant, with solemn promises and the pledge of all they possess—their very hearts and minds, all their days and all their dreams. . . .

In matters of human intimacy, you must wait! You must wait until you can give everything, and you cannot give everything until you are legally and lawfully married. If you persist in pursuing physical satisfaction without the sanction of heaven, you run the terrible risk of such spiritual, psychic damage that you may undermine both your longing for physical intimacy and your ability to give wholehearted devotion to a later, truer love. You may discover to your horror that what you should have saved you have spent, and that only God's grace can recover the virtue you so casually gave away. On your wedding day the very best gift you can give your eternal companion is your very best self—clean and pure and worthy of such purity in return.[4]

Dating right means dating with purity. Unfortunately, many singles—even Latter-day Saint singles—give in to the temptation to engage in intimate relationships. Often such practices are recommended by those of the world as "important" in getting to know your potential spouse in order to gauge chemistry before you get to the altar. They even warn that without such physical expressions of lust, you cannot know whether you are truly compatible. The problem with such thinking is that it's wrong and stupid. It's wrong because the prophets have always warned against such behavior. It's stupid because it discards the Spirit of God from that relationship, and invites Satan to have his way with couples engaged in such behaviors.

The Levels of Love

Love is built in levels. As the following illustrates, physical affection is at the top level, and should not be pursued first. If people pursue physical affection before building a friendship and courting, they set themselves up for large-scale disasters, like the tragedy of being in a serious relationship with or even married to someone they're not even interested in! Can you imagine? Sounds like a recipe for experiencing the fiery depths of hell on earth.

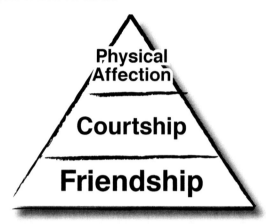

Build a friendship first, before courtship. Sometimes this can be done fairly quickly, but it is definitely necessary. You don't want to date just anyone. Getting feedback from friends and family is often helpful, especially when your family and friends care deeply about your spiritual growth. Courtship begins as you pair off and begin spending time together. And physical affection naturally flows from the fulfillment of friendship and courtship. In other words, without friendship, courtship is not really possible. Why would someone want to spend heart-thumping evenings with someone they don't even like? Furthermore, without friendship and courtship, physical affection is nothing more than lust.

All great marriages are built on the foundation of friendship. And dating is the precious time that you must dedicate to building a lasting friendship. If your friendship is not built on solid ground during the dating process, it must be built in marriage, and that is much more difficult, even impossible for some. Such situations often end in divorce. Couples become enemies because they were never really friends to begin with. Brother John D. Claybaugh wrote the following:

> There is another challenge common to courtships: curbing the desire for premature romantic involvement is an important part of building a strong friendship during dating. Besides being contrary to the commandments of God, physical intimacy before marriage also blocks the development of true friendship. Even the early stages of physical expression of romance can eclipse the mental and spiritual aspects of a relationship and thus halt its progress. Despite what the

world teaches, the highest forms of love are inspired by the Spirit, not by hormones"[5]

Love is simultaneously one of the most sought after and misunderstood things in the world. If love were easy to achieve, all the world would be happy, and there would be no misery or sadness. When true love is embraced, a new life is created.

 All love that has not friendship for its base, is like a mansion built upon the sand.
—Ella Wheeler Wilcox

One of the great tools the Lord has given us is the pamphlet *For the Strength of Youth*. Contrary to what some people think, it is not just for teenagers. This pamphlet is a powerful resource for effective marriage preparation and should be referred to regularly. Countless happily married individuals confirm that it literally saved their spiritual lives from destructive dating habits. In it, the Brethren encourage you to "keep yourself sexually pure. Do not have any sexual relations before marriage. Do not participate in talk or activities that arouse sexual feelings. Do not participate in homosexual activities. Seek help if you become a victim of rape, incest, or other sexual abuse."[6]

Remember that no matter how righteous or good you think you are, you always need to be on your guard in order to avoid making shortsighted mistakes that would ruin your opportunity for blessings. If you are a returned missionary who served valiantly, then that's all the more reason for Satan and his forces to target you. You may have faced severe temptation before, but new pressure and adversity will inevitably rise as you progress spiritually. In other words, the promise of "opposition in all things" (2 Nephi 2:11) is a guarantee that means you will face real opposition, and it may not be easy to overcome. In the case of the Savior's life, that meant facing Satan one-on-one, literally defending the kingdom in a setting where the stakes could not have been any higher, where the salvation of every being to ever exist hung in the balance in those crucial moments.

Though our situations are obviously not so weighty, it remains in our best interest to stand with the Savior because he overcame Satan in all moral matters. We need to position ourselves on high ground, no matter how unpopular that may be to anyone, even some so-called "friends." We can learn from the challenge Paul gave to the Saints at Ephesus to put on the armor of God:

> Put on the whole armour of God, that ye may be able to stand against the wiles of the devil.
>
> For we wrestle not against flesh and blood, but against principalities, against powers, against the rulers of the darkness of this world, against spiritual wickedness in high places.
>
> Wherefore take unto you the whole armour of God, that ye may be able to withstand in the evil day, and having done all, to stand.
>
> Stand therefore, having your loins girt about with truth, and having on the breastplate of righteousness;
>
> And your feet shod with the preparation of the gospel of peace;
>
> Above all, taking the shield of faith, wherewith ye shall be able to quench all the fiery darts of the wicked.
>
> And take the helmet of salvation, and the sword of the Spirit, which is the word of God:
>
> Praying always with all prayer and supplication in the Spirit, and watching thereunto with all perseverance and supplication for all saints (Ephesians 6:11–18).

In all of your dating efforts, remember that you were sent to earth at a very specific time by a Heavenly Father who loves you and who has given you the power of love for a great purpose. Remember, too, that the powers of procreation are not inherently evil. They simply have a time and a place for proper use, and it is not before marriage. Parley P. Pratt said:

> Some persons have supposed that our natural affections were the results of a fallen and corrupt nature, and that they are "carnal, sensual, and devilish," and therefore ought to be resisted, subdued, or overcome as so many evils which prevent our perfection, or progress in the spiritual life. In short, that they should be greatly subdued in this world, and in the world to come entirely done away. And even our intelligence also.
>
> So far from this being the case, our natural affections are planted in us by the Spirit of God, for a wise purpose; and they are the very mainsprings of life and happiness—they are the cement of all virtuous and heavenly society—they are the essence of charity, or love; and therefore never fail, but endure forever.
>
> These pure affections are inspired in our bosoms, and interwoven

with our nature by an all-wise and benevolent being, who rejoices in the happiness and welfare of his creatures. All his revelations to man, touching this subject, are calculated to approve, encourage, and strengthen these emotions, and to increase and perfect them; that man, enlightened and taught of God, may be more free, more social, cheerful, happy, kind, familiar, and lovely than he was before, that he may fill all the relationships of life, and act in every sphere of usefulness of greater energy, and with a readier mind, and a more willing heart.

What then is sinful? I answer, our unnatural passions and affections, or in other words the abuse, the perversion, the unlawful indulgence of that which is otherwise good. Sodom was not destroyed for their natural affections, but for the want of it. They had perverted all their affections, and had given place to that which was unnatural, and contrary to nature. Thus they had lost those holy and pure principles of virtue and love which were calculated to preserve and exalt mankind; and were overwhelmed in all manner of corruption, and also hatred towards those who were good.[7]

Think and Dress Modestly

Those in Church leadership are very aware of the perils that surround the family. Elder L. Tom Perry said, "As we take a long, hard look at the world today, it is becoming increasingly evident that Satan is working overtime to enslave the souls of men. His main target is the fundamental unit of society—the family. During the past few decades, Satan has waged a vigorous campaign to belittle and demean this basic and most important of all organizations."[8]

Satan is attacking the family every day. But what does that mean for those who are dating? Satan is interested in sharing his misery. But he doesn't try to destroy people all at once. Satan doesn't often try, for example, to get a good single Latter-day Saint to commit fornication all of a sudden. Instead, Satan tries to seduce that person into thinking that evil is good, to embrace immodesty, pornography, and thoughts about sex. The prophet Nephi warned us of Satan's tricks when he said, "And there are also secret combinations, even as in times of old, according to the combinations of the devil, for he is the founder of all these things; yea, the founder of murder, and works of darkness; yea, and he leadeth them by the neck with a flaxen cord, until he bindeth them with his strong cords forever" (2 Nephi 26:22).

Although Satan has no power to control our thoughts, he always

CHRIS & JULIA DEAVER AND DON MCCARTNEY

tries to tempt us to think bad things so that we will choose to do bad things. In other words, your greatest battles always start in your mind. Our thoughts are like actors on the stage of our minds—we always have the ability to hire or fire them. Thoughts lead to actions. A wise man once said, "Sow a thought, reap an action; sow an action, reap a habit; sow a habit, reap a destiny."

King Benjamin testified of the influence of our thoughts on our final judgment experience when he said, "But this much I can tell you, that if ye do not watch yourselves, and your thoughts, and your words, and your deeds, and observe the commandments of God, and continue in the faith of what ye have heard concerning the coming of our Lord, even unto the end of your lives, ye must perish. And now, O man, remember, and perish not" (Mosiah 4:30).

One of Satan's areas of expertise is that of immodesty. Satan has made it seem acceptable in the world for people to wear tight-fitting, provocative clothes. As the battle for righteousness rages on, the Brethren repeatedly counsel men and women to dress modestly. Some people may feel that this takes away their individuality and independence, but it really liberates them because they are free to focus on what really matters in this life: developing character and cultivating meaningful relationships with family, friends, and associates.

Chris shares the following experience:

> I still remember being single and going out with a girl who I worked with. She was attractive and an active member of the Church, so I asked her out. We went to dinner. After talking a bit about our backgrounds and educational interests, we discussed some things related to the Church. At one point, she mentioned that she gets frustrated with the constraints and rules of modesty in the Church, and that such expectations are really too demanding. At that point, the date was over. I expressed my feelings about how important following the Prophet in terms of modesty is, and then abruptly ended the conversation, took her home, and never went out with her again. Her attitude was reflective of a bumper sticker that might say, "I Follow the Prophet EXCEPT When He Talks About My Wardrobe."

Sometimes in such situations as immodesty, it may be tempting to some people to "soften" the doctrine, or explain away the Lord's commands by discussing exceptions to the rules, and focusing solely on those. This strategy of down-playing evil in the name of freedom and personal choice are popular but not condoned by the Lord or His prophets. Prophets have always been clear with regard to modesty and virtue. And no amount of discussion on our part will ever change God's laws.

> " " ... | Modesty is not only an ornament, but also a guard to virtue. —Joseph Addison

The Lord has declared that He "delights in the chastity of women" (Jacob 2:28). Though it does not excuse men from their personal responsibility, women who dress modestly help men control their thoughts and be chaste. This, in turn, helps men to see women for the good qualities they possess and to be more appreciative of their inward values. Deeper relationships are built on the basis of more than just a person's outward appearance. And let's face it: aging is a part of life for all of us. Looks will fade as the years go by and wrinkles pile on, but what remains in the heart and soul will be there forever. Plus, would anyone truly want to be totally dependent on personal looks to get their way?

One woman lived her life in precisely this way. She had won a state beauty queen contest because she was physically attractive. After that, she always demanded the highest treatment, without providing kindness herself. In other words, she treated people bitterly and expected people to treat her kindly. The result? She grew up to be an old woman who was no longer able to rely on her physical beauty to get her way, and she later died a sad, single, wrinkled, friendless old maid.

Women who dress modestly help raise the level of respect with which men treat them. Men can then focus on truly getting to know and understand the essence of a woman's soul instead of centering their attention purely on a woman's physical attributes. The selfishness of men seeking momentary gratification will be replaced with a selflessness to serve and love the woman whom they are courting. Amazing relationships can then develop when the foundation of long-term happiness replaces short-term satisfaction as a basis for a friendship or relationship.

One simple, common sense action that makes long-term happiness possible is to avoid getting too physical in a dating relationship. Lying down with each other, even if it starts off innocently, can lead to shameful wickedness. Pain, bitterness, and frustration are the fruits of making this mistake. Potential temple marriages are ruined or delayed on the basis of diminished self-control that occurred between a dating couple.

Guys need to compliment the women they date about things other than physical appearance. Of course, it is nice to tell a woman that you find her beautiful and attractive. But when that is the only reason why you are dating her, it is best to reevaluate if you should proceed in pursuing her. As a man looks inside a woman's heart and sees the things that really matter most, such as her service-minded attitude, excellent communications skills, or faithfulness in attending her church responsibilities, it will be much easier for him to "let virtue garnish [his] thoughts unceasingly" and receive the blessing that his "confidence [will] wax strong in the presence of God" (D&C 121:45).

Jenn S. describes her experience: "I used to spend hours getting ready for a date if I really liked the guy. I'd put on my make-up, pluck my eyebrows, and go tanning. Now I am much less concerned with the physical appearance, so I wish I would have known that that is really marginal and if someone cares too much about that then they aren't worth getting to know anyway."

Don says:

> I cannot tell you how many times, especially when I was attending college that my home teaching companion and I received calls from one of the women we home taught, asking for a blessing. Usually [these calls] came with little warning and often they occurred in the middle of the night or at other random times. When an event like this occurs, priesthood holders should not have to doubt whether they are living worthy enough to give a blessing. Hope and confidence should be the feelings that a priesthood holder has as he participates or gives a blessing. These feelings come from leading a life of integrity and honor. They come from keeping oneself unspotted from the corrupting influences of the world.

There are many books, magazines, and movies that are wholesome and uplifting. Conversely there are many media-driven sources that will pollute and destroy one's senses through the graphic sexual, violent, or profanity-laced material that they contain. The prophet has repeatedly warned us of the tragedies that occur when men allow themselves to indulge in pornographic material. When we rise above the filth, we become people of honor and virtue. We will receive the revelation and direction that we need while giving or receiving a blessing. We will have the Spirit with us. We will be a force for good in the lives of those with whom we come in contact.

Kiss with Caution

-Afraid I was gonna leave without giving you a good-bye kiss?
-I'd just as soon kiss a Wookiee.
-I can arrange that. You could use a good kiss.
—Han Solo & Princess Leia, *Empire Strikes Back*

It is important that during every phase of dating and courtship you look toward the ultimate and eternal goal: a happy and blessed temple marriage. Marriage permits you to practice roles and virtues necessary for eternal life. President Lorenzo Snow related the blessings that can come from such a marriage:

> When two Latter-day Saints are united together in marriage, promises are made to them concerning their offspring that reach from eternity to eternity. They are promised that they shall have the power and the right to govern and control and administer salvation and exaltation and glory to their offspring worlds without end. And what offspring they do not have here, undoubtedly there will be opportunities to have them hereafter. What else could man wish? A man and a woman in the other life, having celestial bodies, free from sickness and disease, glorified and beautified beyond description, standing in the midst of their posterity, governing and controlling them, administering life, exaltation and glory, worlds without end![9]

To stay focused on the eternal blessing of exaltation, you need to commit to only decent acts of affection. Along those lines, what does a kiss mean? Is it just a flimsy, cheap thing with no meaning? Not surprisingly, how we kiss, when we kiss, and whom we kiss are all very important matters to the Lord. Is passionate kissing acceptable before marriage? President Spencer W. Kimball taught:

> Kissing has been prostituted and has degenerated to develop and express lust instead of affection, honor, and admiration. To kiss in casual dating is asking for trouble. What do kisses mean when given out like pretzels and robbed of sacredness? What is miscalled the "soul kiss" is an abomination and stirs passions to the eventual loss of virtue. Even if timely courtship justifies the kiss it should be a clean, decent, sexless

one like the kiss between mother and son, or father and daughter.

If the "soul kiss" with its passion were eliminated from dating there would be an immediate upswing in chastity and honor, with fewer illegitimate babies, fewer unwed mothers, fewer forced marriages, fewer unhappy people. With the absence of the "soul kiss" necking would be greatly reduced. The younger sister of petting, it should be totally eliminated. Both are abominations in their own right.

Immorality does not begin in adultery or perversion. It begins with little indiscretions like sex thoughts, sex discussions, passionate kissing, petting, and such, growing with every exercise. The small indiscretion seems powerless compared to the sturdy body, the strong mind, the sweet spirit of youth who give way to the first temptation. But soon the strong has become weak, the master the slave, spiritual growth curtailed. But if the first unrighteous act is never given root, the tree will grow to beautiful maturity and the youthful life will grow toward God, our Father.[10]

Why do we keep these commandments? Why do we stay moral and clean, and behave in righteousness before the Lord, even when it comes to something as simple as kissing? It is for our happiness. The Lord revealed: "And moreover, I would desire that ye should consider on the blessed and happy state of those that keep the commandments of God. For behold, they are blessed in all things, both temporal and spiritual; and if they hold out faithful to the end they are received into heaven, that thereby they may dwell with God in a state of *never-ending happiness*. O remember, remember that these things are true; for the Lord God hath spoken it" (Mosiah 2:41, emphasis added).

Avoid Pornography

For behold, the Spirit of Christ is given to every man, that he may know good from evil; wherefore, I show unto you the way to judge; for every thing which inviteth to do good, and to persuade to believe in Christ, is sent forth by the power and gift of Christ; wherefore ye may know with a perfect knowledge it is of God.

But whatsoever thing persuadeth men to do evil, and believe not in Christ, and deny him, and serve not God, then ye may know with a perfect knowledge it is of the devil; for after this manner doth the devil work, for he persuadeth no man to do good, no, not one; neither do his angels; neither do they who subject themselves unto him. (Moroni 7:16–17)

Pornography is a destructive influence that is sweeping over the world like a plague. Just like AIDS or other such diseases, it not only destroys its victims, but can kill and seriously desensitize those in its path. Priesthood holders in particular need to be extremely cautious about what they see on television, in movies, and on the Internet. Sometimes what disguises itself as innocent entertainment is actually pornography. Todd had a roommate who put up posters one day of women in bathing suits on his walls. Knowing that such things would only add to his temptation instead of helping him keep his thoughts focused on righteousness, Todd confronted his roommate. In the conversation, Todd mentioned to his roommate how such images of "mild" pornography create a spiritual barrier for someone who is seeking to do God's will. Fortunately, his roommate listened and took down the posters. When in such situations, do as Todd did, and you will be blessed.

Here is a common scenario: a young single adult woman is enraptured and excited about dating a wonderful young man. This woman has spent countless hours going to dinners and watching movies with a man, only to be painfully disappointed in the end by a horrible revelation: the young man she has been dating is addicted to pornography. One such woman had dated a guy for several months. His parents were great people, he had served a mission, and he had achieved great things. But having found out by chance that the guy she was dating was addicted to pornography, she felt strongly compelled by the Spirit to never see him again. She knew that such self-destructive behavior destroys the spiritual senses of an individual unless he repents, and that pornography quickly leads to such things as abuse and adultery.

In a sad turn of events, pornography turns a potential "Prince Charming" into a "Prince Pitiful." This is not to say that one who is addicted to pornography can't change. He surely can. But one should never enter into a dating arrangement with such a person until and unless he has repented fully. And even then, there should be an awareness that he could fall back into that addiction if he is not careful.

So, as a single woman, how can you know when or if the man you are interested in is, in fact, involved in such things? It is not easy to tell. Even his own parents may not know of his hidden, destructive addiction. That is why you need to be extremely careful about whom you choose to date, and why the Spirit is so important in dating. If you pray constantly for the guidance of the Spirit, and allow it to lead you, you will be led in the right way that you should go. If that means breaking up with someone you don't even know that well yet, do it. Do whatever the Spirit tells you to do.

Men, be wise. Don't think that because you served an incredible full-time mission that you will not be tempted. You will be tempted, but you must rise above it. Sometimes movies and the Internet may throw stimulating images at you without you choosing to see them. At such times, you must be strong and turn the computer or television off immediately, or change the channel. Walk out of the theater if you have to. No one will hate you for it. If they do, that's their problem, not yours. Heavenly Father will sustain you. Counseling us against the evils of pornography, Elder Dallin H. Oaks declared the following:

> Do all that you can to avoid pornography. If you ever find yourself in its presence—which can happen to anyone in the world in which we live—follow the example of Joseph of Egypt. When temptation caught him in her grip, he left temptation and "got him out" (Gen. 39:12).
>
> Don't accommodate any degree of temptation. Prevent sin and avoid having to deal with its inevitable destruction. So, turn it off! Look away! Avoid it at all costs. Direct your thoughts in wholesome paths. Remember your covenants and be faithful in temple attendance. The wise bishop I quoted earlier reported that "an endowed priesthood bearer's fall into pornography never occurs during periods of regular worship in the temple; it happens when he has become casual in his temple worship."[11]

Prepare Properly

Some single people think they can keep one foot in the Lord's door and the other in the world's door without any repercussions. Nothing could be further from the truth. One simply cannot hold onto the precious fruit of eternal life while sitting in the great and spacious building. Proper preparation for marriage requires dating that involves being spiritually minded, putting off the natural man, and engaging in Spirit-filled experiences.

Consider this counsel: "O, my beloved brethren, remember the awfulness in transgressing against that Holy God, and also the awfulness of yielding to the enticings of that cunning one. Remember, to be carnally-minded is death, and *to be spiritually-minded is life eternal*" (2 Nephi 9:39, emphasis added). Notice that the words "spiritually-minded is life eternal" spell S-M-I-L-E. True, shining, powerful smiles come only through keeping the Lord's commandments.

Simply put, the happiest marriages are those in which two individuals have come together as they have lived the principles of the gospel of Jesus Christ, in total honesty before the Lord. In *True to the Faith*, the brethren counsel:

> If you are single, prepare yourself carefully for marriage. Remember that there is no substitute for marrying in the temple. Prepare to marry the right person in the right place at the right time. Live worthy now of the kind of person you hope to marry.
>
> Date only those who have high standards and in whose company you can maintain your high standards. Carefully plan positive and constructive activities so that you and your date are not left alone without anything to do. Stay in areas of safety where you can easily control yourself. Do not participate in conversations or activities that arouse sexual feelings.
>
> Look for a companion of your own faith. Look for someone you can always honor and respect, someone who will complement you in your life. Before you marry, be sure you have found someone to whom you can give your entire heart, your entire love, your entire allegiance, your entire loyalty.[12]

Finding the right person is an important part of the equation for a successful marriage, but it also involves preparing yourself as completely as possible. Personal preparation needs to be such that it faces the reality of the challenges of today. One cannot simply approach the problems and situations in this world with an outdated mind-set. It requires so much more than that, more than just wishing or hoping that something great will happen. President Thomas S. Monson shared:

> We live in a changing world. Technology has altered nearly every aspect of our lives. We must cope with these advances—even these cataclysmic changes—in a world of which our forebears never dreamed. Remember the promise of the Lord: "If ye are prepared ye shall not fear." Fear is a deadly enemy of progress.
>
> It is necessary to prepare and to plan so that we don't fritter away our lives. Without a goal, there can be no real success. One

of the best definitions of success I have ever heard goes something like this: success is the progressive realization of a worthy ideal. Someone has said the trouble with not having a goal is that you can spend your life running up and down the field and never cross the goal line.

Years ago there was a romantic and fanciful ballad that contained the words, "Wishing will make it so / Just keep on wishing and care will go." I want to state here and now that wishing will not replace thorough preparation to meet the trials of life. Preparation is hard work but absolutely essential for our progress.

Our journey into the future will not be a smooth highway stretching from here to eternity. Rather, there will be forks and turnings in the road, to say nothing of the unanticipated bumps. We must pray daily to a loving Heavenly Father, who wants each of us to succeed in life.

Prepare for the future.[13]

....

1. Charles W. Dahlquist II, "Who's On the Lord's Side?" *Ensign*, May 2007, 95.

2. Dawn Eden, "The Thrill of the Chaste: In Defense of Sexless Dating," *Today*, March 2, 2008. http://www.msnbc.msn.com/id/23437024/

3. Jeffrey R. Holland, "Personal Purity," *New Era*, Feb. 2000, 4.

4. Ibid.

5. John D. Claybaugh, "Dating: A Time to Become Best Friends," *Ensign*, Apr. 1994, 19.

6. *For the Strength of Youth* [card] (Salt Lake City: Intellectual Reserve, 2001), 1.

7. Parley P. Pratt, "Intelligence and Affection," from *The Writings of Parley P. Pratt*, quoted by Truman J. Madsen in *4 Essays on Love* (Salt Lake City: Deseret Book, 2007), 34–36.

8. L. Tom Perry, "Fatherhood, an Eternal Calling," *Ensign*, May 2004.

9. Lorenzo Snow, "Remarks," *Deseret Weekly,* April 3, 1897.

10. Spencer W. Kimball, *The Teachings of Spencer W. Kimball*, Edited by Edward L. Kimball (Salt Lake City: Bookcraft, 1982).

11. Dallin H. Oaks, "Pornography," *Ensign*, May 2005, 87

12. *True to the Faith,* [pamphlet] (Salt Lake City: The Church of Jesus Christ of Latter-day Saints, 2004,) 98–99.

13. Thomas S. Monson, "Treasure of Eternal Value," *Ensign*, Apr. 2008, 2–7.

Week Seven Commitment: Commit to keep all of the Lord's commandments with respect to morality. Decide what you can do to increase your discipleship. Share that commitment with the Lord, and repent if necessary.

What I Need to Do to Better Keep the Commandments

_____

_____

_____

_____

_____

_____

_____

_____

_____

_____

_____

_____

_____

_____

_____

_____

_____

_____

_____

Part 3:

The Next Level

8

Serve Selflessly

Treating Your Date like Royalty

Total unselfishness is sure to accomplish another factor in successful marriage. If one is forever seeking the interests, comforts, and happiness of the other, the love found in courtship and cemented in marriage will grow into mighty proportions. Certainly the foods most vital for love are consideration, kindness, thoughtfulness, concern, expressions of affection, embraces of appreciation, admiration, pride, companionship, confidence, faith, partnership, equality, and interdependence. —President Spencer W. Kimball[1]

Before you go on a date, seriously consider how you will bless the life of the fair maiden or prince charming with whom you will spend a few precious hours. Don't worry so much about yourself. Get lost in thinking about the other person and how you can serve that person. Think of the other person as real royalty because that person is a son or daughter of God with the full potential to become like our Heavenly Parents. Always remember that.

 Love seeketh not itself to please, nor for itself hath any care, but for another gives its ease, and builds a heaven in hell's despair. —William Blake

When Ammon arrived in the land of the Lamanites to preach the gospel to the people, he didn't first go about commanding them to repent or chase them down to baptize them immediately. He focused first on serving the people, saying to the Lamanite King, "I will be thy servant" (Alma 17:25). As you date, have a heart of service and think constantly on the needs of that special someone with whom you have been so blessed to spend some time.

Selfishness is the surest way to dating destruction. On the other hand, selflessness is the surest way to dating and marriage success. Selflessness is naturally expressed in acts of service and is like oxygen to people's social lives. Reflecting on the power of service to bless lives, including our own, King Benjamin asserted, "And behold, I tell you these things that ye may learn wisdom; that ye may learn that when ye are in the service of your fellow beings ye are only in the service of your God" (Mosiah 2:17).

 Love grows by giving. The love we give away is the only love we keep. The only way to retain love is to give it away.
—Elbert Hubbard

Jason M. iterates this point: "There was a time when I only wanted to date just for my own pleasure. But after coming closer to the Savior I realized that I want to get married to spend my life with and support someone, to help her be the best she can possibly be."

Kate V. adds, "On a date, always be more concerned about how the other person is feeling than how you are feeling and focus completely on meeting his or her needs. Other things that I recommend are to look for little ways to serve guys like on their birthday, doing something for them, writing [them] a nice note once in a while, telling them what you appreciate about [them]."

Start now to experience the joy available by serving those you date during courtship. It's easy to go on a date thinking only about your own feelings, thoughts, worries, and expectations. It takes true commitment to the Savior and the goal of exaltation to enter a dating relationship with service in mind. But that is what godhood takes. After all, isn't that what Heavenly Father does for us every day? He serves. He is all about service as He blesses our lives constantly.

Wise singles remember the blessings of kindness. In one of the greatest revelations, the Lord counseled men and women with this powerful advice: "No power or influence can or ought to be maintained by virtue of the priesthood [or by coercion] only by persuasion, by long-suffering, by gentleness and meekness, and by love unfeigned; By kindness, and pure knowledge, which shall greatly enlarge the soul without hypocrisy, and without guile" (D&C 121:41–42).

Speaking on the subject of avoiding divorce, President Gordon B. Hinckley declared,

> Why all of these broken homes? What happens to marriages that begin with sincere love and a desire to be loyal and faithful and true one to another? There is no simple answer. I acknowledge that. But it appears to me that there are some obvious reasons that account for a very high percentage of these problems. I say this out of experience in dealing with such tragedies. I find selfishness to be the root cause of most of it. I am satisfied that a happy marriage is not so much a matter of romance as *it is an anxious concern for the comfort and well-being of one's companion.*"[2]

How can you serve your date? Melissa C. says, "Guys sometimes don't pay girls enough compliments or tell them the things that they appreciate about them or do enough nice things for them. Those are things that go a long way for girls."

Some Acts of Service	
Guys	**Girls**
Ask her out several days in advance	Accept his invitation several days before
Show up on time	Be ready on time
Open doors	Be polite
Pay for the meal/ activity	Thank him for paying
Pay sincere compliments	
Listen Sincerely	
Express appreciation for each other's time and company	

 Love is a fruit in season at all times, and within reach of every hand.
—Mother Teresa

Marcus J. says, "You can't be ego inflated. You can't bank on a prior victory to get you through. You've got to always serve her needs in everything you do."

When you sacrifice for another person in a dating relationship, you build a bond that can last. It is different than superficial feelings of infatuation, in that it shares and creates feelings that are truly Christlike in nature. A research study of multiple dating couples showed that motives for sacrifice in dating were positively associated with personal well-being and relationship quality. Those who avoided sacrificing for their dating partner experienced a general lack of well-being and relationship quality.[3]

 A life's worth, the end isn't measured in hours, or dollars. It's measured by the amount of love exchanged along the way.
—Douglas C. Means

Treating your date like royalty by sacrificing and serving is a philosophy that conflicts with the world's advice to expect everything from your date without necessarily giving anything. But it is nevertheless the only real solution for marriage survival.

Make Manners Matter

It usually doesn't take very long when one is on a date to find out about the other person's manners or lack thereof. If the guy doesn't show you that he has good manners, he might just as well be on a guy's night out. If he doesn't go out of his way to make the evening a special one then it can be very disappointing. Occasionally, there might be a slip up here or there. For instance, maybe he is nervous and accidentally spills water on the table or maybe he is so entranced in conversation with you that he forgets to open a door. If these events occur, they should be overlooked. We are all human and make mistakes. It is the consistent overall pattern that you will want to do right as well as see.

Table manners are always important, whether dining at a fancy restaurant or just sitting down for some fast food. For instance, when the food comes, does she eat like she is at the trough? Does he chew with his mouth open?

Don shares this unfortunate experience: "One of the worst examples of poor manners came on one of the most recent dates that I went on.

The woman left her cell phone on and was constantly checking it the whole date. On the way over to the orchestra she was text messaging her brother. During intermission she received a call and picked it up and spoke for a couple of minutes. It's often the little things that make or break your date or interest in your date."

One thing to look for is how much your date initiates conversation with you. Or does your date constantly talk about old memories or events with friends you don't know. This always makes it more difficult for one to become active in the conversation, even when one has the desire to. After all, the point of being on the date in the first place is to get to know your date better and see if you can build a friendship.

· ·

1. Spencer W. Kimball, "Oneness in Marriage," *Ensign*, March, 1977, 5.
2. Gordon B. Hinckley, "What God Hath Joined Together," *Ensign*, May 1991, 71, emphasis added.
3. Emily A. Impett, Shelly L Gable, and Letitia Anne Peplau, "Giving Up and Giving In: The Costs and Benefits of Daily Sacrifice in Intimate Relationships, *Journal of Personality and Social Psychology* 89, no. 3 (2005) 327–44.

Week Eight Commitment: Determine three specific ways you will serve the next person you go on a date with, and then do them.

1. _____

_____

_____

_____

_____

_____

2. _____

_____

_____

_____

_____

_____

3. _____

_____

_____

_____

_____

_____

_____

9

Court Continuously

Wooing in the Name of Love

Wherefore, my beloved brethren, pray unto the Father with all the energy of heart, that ye may be filled with this love, which he hath bestowed upon all who are true followers of his Son, Jesus Christ; that ye may become the sons of God; that when he shall appear we shall be like him, for we shall see him as he is; that we may have this hope; that we may be purified even as he is pure. Amen. —Moroni 7:48

Charity is the greatest of all, and it never fails. Date with charity, and you will never fail. Yes, there may be setbacks. And, no, you may not find your eternal companion immediately. But as you "pray unto the Father with all the energy of heart" for the gift of charity, you will receive a sublime power that strengthens you.

Date with Charity and Never Fail

Charity has been defined as "the pure love of Christ" (Moroni 7:47). Charity is so important that in 2 Nephi 26:30, Nephi tells us, "And except they should have charity they were nothing."

 He who gives money gives some, he who gives time gives more, but he who gives of himself gives all.
—President Thomas S. Monson[1]

What does it mean to give of oneself? One of the most readily apparent answers is in seeking for the welfare and happiness of your date. No matter what your wants and desires are, your focus needs to include the long-term happiness of your date.

 They do not love that do not show their love.
—William Shakespeare

Regarding charity in dating, Jake D. mentions, "I have known girls who were really caring, who would remember things that were going on in my life and ask me about them. I could tell that they sincerely cared about me as a person. And that level of charity matters to me."

John had dated Marie for several weeks. He was impressed by her spirituality, love for family, and desire to be a good wife and mother. During spring vacation, Marie went home to visit her family for a week. John missed her instantly. He talked to his roommates and friends about the prospect of him driving hundreds of miles to her home just to visit her. Each friend had different advice. Some said he should wait until she called him. Others told him to call her first, wait a day, and then call her again. John felt confused by the advice, so he went to the scriptures. He read in Moroni 7:46, "For charity never faileth." That scripture impacted John's heart, and he knew what he needed to do.

John realized that if he were exercising charity in his actions, that whatever he did would be aligned with the Lord's will for him. He knew that his course was to show his love to Marie. So he drove the hundreds of miles to visit Marie, and he met her family. This became a building experience for them as they courted and married soon after.

 I want to know God's thoughts; the rest are details.
—Albert Einstein

Often the Lord's instructions include the principles of faith, hope, and charity. How we choose to apply those principles becomes a very personal approach. We are to be anxiously engaged.

Brother Ken Shelton, world-class author and editor said:

> We seek to find a loving mate and procreate and certainly we give high priority to these and other family relationships. Nonetheless we maintain a mission orientation, meaning that we remain open to personal guidance regarding our next steps, even if that means: a)

marrying someone who is "different" from our parents' expectations (perhaps someone of another culture or country); b) having a family that is "different" from the "model" family; or c) taking that spouse and family on an adventure that is "different" from a traditional career or local "hometown" lifestyle. Often, having a mission orientation in marriage and family matters means making choices and decisions that are painful, unpopular, and misunderstood. In fact, you may not even understand why you are so choosing, except that it's common in service and sacrifice not to know everything up front.[2]

In dating, building a relationship to last not only takes time and persistence, but it takes the right thinking. That is, it takes thinking about the other person as much as possible and building the relationship.

Woo, Woo, Woo

What does it mean to "woo"? It means to do something special for someone you like, something that demonstrates kindness, sincerity, and love. It is important to woo because it helps your date to experience feelings of love. Love is a verb. It requires action. And wooing is the expression of love.

The meter below was designed to demonstrate the effects of wooing with a particular activity.

Woo-O-Meter

Score "Woo Points" with these simple gestures	
Share a genuine compliment	1 point
Write a nice text, email, or card	5 points
Deliver flowers or baked goods	5 points
Share a romantic dinner	7 points
Be the first to call on his or her birthday	7 points
Take him or her to their favorite activity	8 points
Give a special, personalized gift	9 points
Tell him or her "I love you"	10 points
Share an appropriate and timely kiss, hug, or hand-hold	10 points

 The best and most beautiful things in this world cannot be seen or even heard, but must be felt with the heart.
—Helen Keller

In his book *The Wednesday Letters*, bestselling author Jason F. Wright tells the story of Jack and Laurel who have been married for thirty-nine years and seem to have had the perfect marriage. In order to share his love for his wife, Jack wrote her a "Wednesday Letter" every week. This practice of wooing through the written word can certainly make a difference in dating and in marriage. It is a sign of thoughtfulness, love, and appreciation.[3]

 If you want something to last forever, you treat it differently . . . It becomes special because you have made it so.
—F. Burton Howard

True love is powerful. The restored gospel of Jesus Christ teaches us about that true love. Scholar Truman G. Madsen said:

> Love is Fire. That is the great secret. It is Fire with a large F. It is Divine Fire. When it is in you it lights you, all of you. And transforms. No self-induced flicker can compare with it.
>
> Modern revelation has several words for the emanation that conveys this Love. They are not exact synonyms: Live. Light. Spirit. Power. All are "sent forth by the will of the Father through Jesus Christ His Son."
>
> Thus you cannot "make love." You cannot love until you are loved. You cannot be loved until you are Beloved. Beloved of God. His flame burns and encircles reaching the self at its core, its spiritual center, and then moving outward to physical fingers and toes. Such love, over long periods, becomes diamond-like. A real diamond, being pure carbon, burns up in split seconds surrounded by flame. Yet there are other fantastic pressures and refinements that give it luster and sheen until it can cut and endure through almost anything. Love in you is both that destructible and that durable.[4]

Love and Be Loved

 Some pray to marry the man they love, my prayer will somewhat vary: I humbly pray to heaven above that I love the man I marry.—Anouk Aimee

What does it mean to truly love someone? Have you ever done it before? Most singles admit that they haven't (yet). What is love, anyway? Is it simply something that we have because its been built into our biological systems, or is it a truly powerful verb that we can apply to accomplish incredible things? Researchers have done studies to find out, and this is some of what they've found:

> Tom Holman, BYU professor of family life, disagrees with the idea of love simply being an evolutionary process. Instead, Holman argues that it was placed in humans by God starting with Adam and Eve. In addition, Holman explained how love is manifest differently depending on the person and his or her life situation, which suggests how and what people love is a choice, not a force of evolution. Humans develop love through a series of connections, or "attachments," with other human beings from infancy to adulthood. "By our very natures, we seek connections with other people. That first attachment is usually with a parent . . . a mother," Holman said. "If it's done well, we feel secure, we feel confident and competent."
>
> Holman explained further that if the attachment does not take place, the child can feel insecure and scared, attributes that they carry into adulthood. However, humans can choose to overcome insecurities and have healthy relationships as adults, or keep their insecurities and develop immature relationships. Either way, it is up to the individual, not evolution.
>
> Holman defined love as the security and trust that begins in infancy with healthy attachments and progresses into a mature love as an adult: a love that entails friendship, sharing and fulfillment of needs, both physical and emotional. "In movies we see sexual lust, but that isn't love," Holman said. "Our culture wants you to believe that is what love is, that you can satisfy these sexual things and then a more mature love will grow out of it. Research doesn't support that, but movie makers don't care about research."[5]

Achieve Your Potential

> And again, verily I say unto you, if a man marry a wife by my word, which is my law, and by the new and everlasting covenant, and it is sealed unto them by the Holy Spirit of promise, by him who is anointed, unto whom I have appointed this power and the keys of this priesthood; and it shall be said unto them—Ye shall come forth in the first resurrection; and if it be after the first resurrection, in the next resurrection; and shall inherit thrones, kingdoms, principalities, and powers, dominions, all heights and depths—then shall it be written in the Lamb's Book of Life, that he shall commit no murder

whereby to shed innocent blood, and if ye abide in my covenant, and commit no murder whereby to shed innocent blood, it shall be done unto them in all things whatsoever my servant hath put upon them, in time, and through all eternity; and shall be of full force when they are out of the world; and they shall pass by the angels, and the gods, which are set there, to their exaltation and glory in all things, as hath been sealed upon their heads, which glory shall be a fulness and a continuation of the seeds forever and ever.

Then shall they be gods, because they have no end; therefore shall they be from everlasting to everlasting, because they continue; then shall they be above all, because all things are subject unto them. Then shall they be gods, because they have all power, and the angels are subject unto them (D&C 132:19–20).

Exit Unnecessary Comfort Zones

Comfort zones are funny things. They can be helpful, but comfort zones that keep us from doing great things are never helpful. To break free from worthless comfort zones like the fear of speaking to or wooing the opposite sex, you need to be bold. You need to be willing to experience new things, new emotions, and even new disappointments. Failure is a part of life, and that's okay. And yet, failure is always found along the path to success.

So, talk to the person you are most interested in dating. Go on a date. Be bold and spontaneous and make it fun. Keep moving forward even when things don't seem exactly the way you want them to be. Often life will bring disappointments. It's what we do with those that matters. Do we give up? No, we put our shoulder to the wheel and press on with the faith of our forefathers, not stopping until the promise land is reached.

Be Positive

 Death cannot stop true love. All it can do is delay it for a while.—William Goldman, *The Princess Bride*

Sometimes, when life is tossing lemons at people, the same people react by being sour. Instead of making lemonade, they throw the lemons at someone else by being negative. Negativity is like a sickness, a plague that curses everyone in its path. And when negativity has entered the heart of the dater, happiness becomes impossible. Fortunately, we have been given the power to choose to be positive. Every day, we can wake up and face new opportunities with zeal. When we are positive, we invite the fruits of positive thinking, which are peace, happiness, joy, greater faith, and even miracles. In a study of numerous dating relationships, university researchers confirmed that being positive creates positive results.

> Does expecting positive outcomes—especially in important life domains such as relationships—make these positive outcomes more likely? In a longitudinal study of dating couples, the authors tested whether optimists (who have a cognitive disposition to expect positive outcomes) and their romantic partners are more satisfied in their relationships, and if so, whether this is due to optimists perceiving greater support from their partners. In cross-sectional analyses, both optimists and their partners indicated greater relationship satisfaction, an effect that was mediated by optimists' greater perceived support. When the couples engaged in a conflict conversation, optimists and their partners saw each other as engaging more constructively during the conflict, which in turn led both partners to feel that the conflict was better resolved one week later. In a one-year follow-up, men's optimism predicted relationship status. Effects of optimism were mediated by the optimists' perceived support, which appears to promote a variety of beneficial processes in romantic relationships.[6]

Stay positive regardless of circumstances and you will find greater joy. You will achieve what you and the Lord want for you.

∙∙∙∙∙∙∙∙∙∙∙∙∙∙∙∙∙∙∙∙∙∙

1. Thomas S. Monson, "The Gifts of Christmas," *Ensign,* Dec. 2003, 2–5.
2. Ken Shelton, interviewed by the authors.
3. Jason F. Wright, *The Wednesday Letters* (Salt Lake City: Shadow Mountain, 2007).
4. Truman G. Madsen, *Four Essays on Love* (Salt Lake City: Deseret Book, 2007).
5. Elizabeth Gosney, "The Evolution of Human Love," *The Daily Universe,* February 13, 2008.
6. James J. Gross, Kelly M. McGonigal, Sanjay Srivastava, Jane M. Richards, and Emily A. Butler, "Optimism in Close Relationships: How Seeing Things in a Positive Light Makes Them So," *Journal of Personality and Social Psychology* 91, no. 1 (2006), 143–53.

Week Nine Commitment: Pray for the gift of charity and woo someone by being positive and doing something special for that person.

My Plan of When to Pray for the Gift of Charity:

_____

_____

_____

_____

_____

_____

_____

_____

_____

What I Will Do to Woo Someone Special:

_____

_____

_____

_____

_____

_____

_____

_____

_____

_____

_____

_____

_____

_____

10

Communicate Honestly

Talking Straight from the Heart

And they were among the people of Nephi, and also numbered among the people who were of the church of God. And they were also distinguished for their zeal towards God, and also towards men; for they were perfectly honest and upright in all things; and they were firm in the faith of Christ, even unto the end. —Alma 27:27, emphasis added

Some people pretend to be someone they are not. They say things that are incongruent with what they really are. This ultimately gets them into trouble and creates major frustration for their dates. Being your genuine self is an attractive attribute to have. Remember, you are the only one of you. You have unique qualities and strengths. No one else can take these from you. As you relax and are true to yourself, you will find that others who are looking for the qualities and characteristics you possess will be attracted to you.

Be sincere

Be authentic with people and you will find people will like you more. You won't have to brag or prove anything. People will sense who you are, respect that, and follow your humble example.

Anna F. says, "I like a man who is sincere. Sincere about wanting to get to know me, sincere about what he tells me his interests are, sincere with how he is as a person."

Being sincere in dating means being honest and straightforward in what you do. For example, you would never want to communicate to someone you did not like that you are in love with him. That would be dishonest. And that's one reason you would have to be careful about what you say and do with that person. Physical expressions of affection are a communication of love and should be wisely and carefully expressed for that reason.

To be sincere, we must remember that by being baptized in the Church of Jesus Christ of Latter-day Saints, we have taken upon ourselves the name of Jesus Christ, and then we must act accordingly. The great prophet Alma elaborated on this principle when he asked, "I say unto you, can ye look up to God at that day with a pure heart and clean hands? I say unto you, can you look up, having the image of God engraven upon your countenances?" (Alma 5:19)

Cindy G. says, "If you are not interested at least be honest. If you get asked out and are truly not at all interested you should say, 'No.' "

Clarissa O. says, "Men are often receptive to physical communication, but that does not always mean that they are on the same level that you are. People can be thinking completely different things. You may kiss and think that you're communicating the same things and you may not be. Physical contact is a very good form of communicating, but you can't communicate everything with it. So you need to make sure that you keep open, honest, sincere communication."

Communicate as You Date

Communication is one of the most essential aspects to any relationship. It is closely related to another key relationship ingredient, that of trust. You don't and won't want to relate highly personal experiences and your inner feelings to someone whom you feel like you can't trust. Dating author John Gray said, "It is not enough to merely be authentic in sharing yourself; to succeed in dating you need to consider how you will be interpreted as well."[1]

Lindsey B. says, "The best dating experiences I have had have always come by communicating honestly and with guys being very open with their feelings, even if they say things that I don't want to hear."

How does one acquire another's trust? There are a few time-proven approaches that have been shown to be successful. Show genuine interest in what members of the opposite sex have to say to you when you are in their company. Don't let your thoughts wander when you are in their presence. Maintain focus on them and what they are telling you. By doing this, you can show them that you value them.

Remember details of conversations that you have. This indicates to the person of the opposite gender that the friendship and the relationship that you have with them is of importance to you. Next time you see them, be sure to bring up a particular topic that they mentioned to you previously. This will help to solidify your friendship and relationship, because they will know that the things that are of relevance to them also have meaning to you.

Another way to build trust is to share personal experiences and feelings. As you do this, the "law of reciprocation," comes into play. People feel and acknowledge that you trust them because you have shared things of importance to you with them. They feel less vulnerable around you and want to return the trust that you have shown them, by sharing their thoughts and feelings with you.

To build trust effectively through communication, you must share the right kind of information at the right time. In the early stages of dating, for example, you should generally avoid talking or asking about past dating relationships. Such things don't make for good conversation pieces because such subjects can create resentment, frustration, or misunderstanding on the part of your date. In one such case, a guy asked his date about a past dating relationship and kept pressing her to give more information until she started crying incessantly. He had brought up a horribly sensitive issue, and in the process, he gave his date a memorable negative experience that left her without any desire to go out with him ever again. Use the **FEEL** approach to try to focus early conversations on such things as:

Family/Friends
Employment
Experiences
Likes

Karla E. states, "Get to know your date and try to understand his or her potential, goals, and so on. Learn to support other people in their interests and dreams."

Define the Relationship

Communication can be compared to driving a car. When you are driving, you want to let the other drivers know what your true intentions are. That is, you need to signal left or right, so they know what you're doing. This not only avoids accidents, but it makes for courteous, trust-building results. Communication in dating is no different.

How do you communicate effectively when you have to talk about tough topics like the future of a dating relationship? Be direct. Don't be afraid to tell the person that you are not interested. Just make sure to do it in a way that you would like to have done to you, if you were in the same situation. Also, make sure that you are not misunderstood. Some girls will keep accepting dates from a guy they have no interest in simply because they don't want to hurt his feelings. "Charity dates" like that end up achieving nothing but disappointment and more painful rejection when the girl finally has to tell the guy that she's really not interested.

Researchers have done studies that demonstrate that it is better to deliver bad news all at once rather than in little pieces. The same goes in dating when you're not interested in someone. Simply let him or her know. But don't be mean about it. The best advice ever offered about dumping in dating was "Be Kind." That is, never forget to treat that person like a son or daughter of Heavenly Father.

 Two such as you with such a master speed / Cannot be parted nor be swept away / From one another once you are agreed / That life is only life forevermore / Together wing to wing and oar to oar.—Robert Frost

Remember that dating is in fact a process of selection. That is, you will only end up with one person. And the person you have your eyes on at any given time will also only end up with one person. So don't let the fact that it may not work out with one person affect the three million or so other chances you have for success. If it doesn't work out, you can still look each other in the eye. You can still talk to him or her in Church. And you can still maintain respect and admiration for him or her. No matter what the other person does, don't ever stoop to backbiting or cutting him or her down with unkind words. Instead, treat others how Christ would treat them.

What about when the dating situation is much more serious? That is, what do you do when you and your date both have strong feelings and one of you needs to close down the dating relationship? What can you do to prevent saying something insensitive or to avoid running away?

There is no question that emotions can run high, especially when you're defining the relationship or doing a "DTR," and trying to figure out together what direction you're both going.

In the context of communication, "start with heart" means to clarify your purpose in the conversation. Before starting the conversation, ask yourself, "What do I really want for myself? What do I really want for others? What do I really want for the relationship?" "Fill the pool of shared meaning" means to ensure that people are sharing their opinions, feelings, theories, and experiences about the topic. "Create safety" means to ensure that people feel comfortable sharing their thoughts without rejection, ridicule, blaming, and so on. "Master your stories" means to make sure that we connect the actions of others with their true motives. Applying these tools has helped many couples in their dating dilemmas.[2]

Do not gossip. It violates trust. If you do have a compelling urge to tell someone else something that was revealed to you in confidence, make sure that you run the idea past the person who told it to you first.

There are two types of communication with which you should be concerned. The first is how well you and your potential significant other can communicate. When we use the word "communicate" we mean more than just carrying on a good conversation with the other person. When you first get to know someone, generally there is a lot to talk about, since everything is new. After you finish discussing the basics (i.e., where are you from, what's your major, what are your hobbies, tell me about your family), then the true test is to see if the two of you feel comfortable conversing about even more serious topics.

Alex H. mentions, "Sometimes there are miscommunication problems between the genders and it is because of different expectations. What exactly does a date mean? Does it mean that we're just trying to get to know each other or does it mean we're genuinely interested in each other? During a date, a girl may be sending signals out that she's interested or she's not and a guy can be totally oblivious to it because he doesn't understand the subtleties of what the girl is doing."

Often it seems that women and men are speaking totally different languages. He is thinking about kissing her, while she is wondering why he isn't listening. She is thinking about the relationship, and he is fixated on how his favorite basketball team performed that night.

Why would a loving Heavenly Father wire us this way? Did he do it so that He could look down at us and get a good laugh as we confuse each other? No. Heavenly Father has *blessed* us with different ways of thinking. When this difference is understood for what it truly is—a blessing—we can open our hearts and minds to be taught from each other and from the Spirit. Consider it this way:

> Problems in relationships come about in essentially two ways. We either think that others actually do see things as we do, so we can't understand or are upset by their reactions—or we believe that others should see things the way we do because we see reality as it really is. When we understand the principle of separate realities we are free from these catalysts of relationship problems. Others not only shouldn't see things our way, but in fact they cannot. The nature of individual thought systems makes it impossible for us to see anything the way someone else does—or for others to see things precisely as we do. This new understanding frees us from a false idea and brings the joy back into our differences. It's one thing to say, "variety is the spice of life," and another to really believe and understand it. The trick in believing this is not to force yourself to think this way, but to see that, from a psychological perspective, differences between people and the ways they see life make complete sense.[3]

In communication, one topic that comes into play is the gospel. How comfortable are you in sharing your testimony with your friend? How about discussing spiritual experiences that are somewhat personal? Since many of us hold our testimonies close to our hearts, we sometimes fear that if we talk about our true thoughts and feelings, others may make fun of us. If you don't feel comfortable sharing your insights and feelings about the gospel with someone you are interested in, it may be time to reevaluate just how far your relationship with that person has progressed. This is not to say that you should prematurely disregard someone you are interested in just because you haven't discussed the gospel in the course of the first few dates. Give it time, but be aware that it is an important factor in determining how well the two of you can and do communicate with each other.

Veronica B. says, "The worst thing about some dates that I have gone on is having to talk about myself the whole time or ask the guy a billion questions because he either won't talk about himself or he won't ask me anything about myself."

Listen, Listen, Listen

 The first duty of love is to listen.
—Anonymous

During the process of getting to know your various interests better, another piece of the communication puzzle to pay attention to is how often your date is asking you questions and probing deeper to find out more about you. Perhaps there have been times when you have come home from a date thinking, "Wow, that was a great conversation," when in reality it was only a *good* conversation. It was good because both people were talking, but not as good as it could have been because one person was generating all the questions and initiating the dialogue. You will find that if you try hard enough and are patient enough, you can have *great* conversations with anyone. Sometimes a good litmus test (though we don't recommend doing it frequently) is to pause when there is a natural break in the conversation and wait for your date to ask you a question. Do this if you feel you have dominated the conversation with your questions and if you have spent enough time with your date to justify using this technique. If there is a prolonged awkward silence, this may be an indicator for you to look elsewhere.

Rick A. adds, "A kind person perceives the needs of others and then acts upon them in a manner that's befitting, whatever needs that others might have. It's important to me that the girl I'm looking for has that quality, that she's perceptive to people's needs. And that she knows how to act on [her perceptions] to best serve others."

Jessica S. says, "If I'm dating someone seriously, I'll offer to pay for the meal or the date that we're going on, as a gesture to say, 'Hey I appreciate the time I spend with you too.' Let him know how you feel about him. I think that does a lot for guys. If you observe them doing something that you are impressed with, make sure you tell them that. All these things help give a guy confidence and help the relationship move forward."

True love comes quietly, without banners or flashing lights. If you hear bells, get your ears checked.
—Erich Segal

Another type of nonverbal communication that you need to pay attention to in the dating game is eye contact. Eye contact is critical because when members of the opposite sex are willing to look you in the eye, it shows you a few things about them. They trust you, they are actually listening, they are paying attention to what you have to say, and they are quite possibly attracted to you.

Don says:

> The doorstep scene is another place where initiating some contact is a good idea especially if you had a genuinely good time. It can serve to put the guy or girl at ease. I have found myself in situations where I was totally baffled by what the girl did. Many times, I have been unsure as to whether she wants to start an in-depth conversation at the door step, say "bye" and then run quickly inside, or if she plans to just ignore me, pretending our date never happened, and unlock their door, disregarding all social graces of saying good night. I remember one date in particular where the girl, though very shy and about a month removed from her mission, pulled out the key to unlock the door and had the key halfway in when I went in for a hug. That was an awkward moment if there ever were one! From then, I decided that it was a good idea to try and be a little bit more observant and read my date better.

Create opportunities for sharing things of great interest to you and your date. If you let them, and you set the right stage, people will freely indulge you in what they are truly passionate about in life. This not only allows them to show you some of their depth, but it can also be used to your advantage. Once you know what hobbies and interests electrify your date, you can suggest the two of you go and participate in that activity at some future time. This way you already have an excuse to go out together again.

Great dating requires great communication. And great communication requires meeting the emotional needs of your date. So often, men and women feel frustrated and unsure about their dating relationship because they are falling sadly short of meeting each other's needs. Men and women each have different needs when it comes to communication. And to the extent that you can meet the needs of your date, you will feel greater love for that person, and you will have greater opportunities for a happy, eternal marriage. Consider these six key points that men and women should follow in communicating effectively:

1. She needs caring and he needs trust.
2. She needs understanding and he needs acceptance.
3. She needs respect and he needs appreciation.
4. She needs devotion and he needs admiration.
5. She needs validation and he needs approval.
6. She needs reassurance and he needs encouragement.[4]

John D. mentions, "Communicating level of interest is a simple thing, but at the same time, interpreting it can be a little bit tricky because one person's flirty is another person's friendly. I don't know that there is a solution for that. I believe that you need to get to know someone better so that you can put how they act around you into context with how they are in general."

Camille A. adds, "I'm not going to sit there and wonder what is he thinking about where we stand, whether we are dating each other exclusively or dating other people. Just ask, and you will save yourself a lot of time."

Hannah E. says, "The most important thing a woman can do is be positive. If she likes a guy, she should be positive, not aggressive. If she had a great night she should call him and say, 'I had a great night, and just want to let you know that I enjoyed it.' By honestly letting yourself positively respond, the guy can pick up on it, and he'll know that you're interested."

The eyes have often been called "the window of the soul." Since most of us daters aren't mind readers, we can identify the expression in our date's eyes to portray a more accurate account of what she is actually thinking than sometimes even what they say. Even if people say yes to something that they're not really interested in doing, their eyes will generally give their thoughts away because they will look away from the person with whom they are speaking either at the ground, another person, or something else.

Avoid Abuse

Even though we all plan for dating relationships that are healthy, the unfortunate truth is that there are some relationships that are—in fact—unhealthy. What do you do if the person you are dating is abusing you verbally, sexually, physically, or otherwise? Do you continue dating him or her, hoping that the person will change? Absolutely not! You get out of the relationship immediately and get the help of whomever you need to do so, whether that's friends, parents, or even the police. Refer often to the following lists[5]:

I have the right to

• Be treated with respect	• Pay my own way
• My own body, thoughts, opinions, and property	• Not be abused physically, emotionally, or sexually
• Have my needs be as important as my partner's needs	• Determine how much time I want to spend with my partner
• Not take responsibility for my partner's behavior	• Break-up, fall out of love, or leave a relationship
• Keep my friends	• Grow as an individual
• Change my mind	• Assert myself

Forms of Abuse

• Physical: actions that cause physical pain or injury, such as kicking, pushing, or punching	• Emotional: actions that cause loss of self-esteem, such as name-calling, swearing, or criticizing
• Psychological: actions that create fear, such as isolations or threats	• Sexual: acts of a sexual nature that are unwelcome or uncomfortable.

Beware of Anger

Even in the LDS dating scene, anger problems can show up. This is something to be aware of. You may even need to dump someone if they have this problem. People with serious character or personality flaws do not suddenly change after marriage. If a person has a problem like anger or abuse, he will likely carry it into marriage with him. And then it will be your problem. So don't let that happen.

••••••••••••••••••••••

1. John Gray, *Mars and Venus on a Date: A Guide for Navigating the 5 Stages of Dating* (New York: Harper, 1999), 3.

2. Kerry Patterson, Joseph Grenny, Ron McMillan and Al Switzler, *Crucial Conversations* (New York: McGraw-Hill, 2002).

3. Richard Carlson, *You Can Be Happy No Matter What* (Novato, CA: New World Library, 1997), 41.

4. John Gray, *Mars and Venus in Touch* (New York: HarperCollins, 1992), 22–23

5. Karianne Salisbury, "Recognizing Red Flags in Relationships," *Daily Universe*, March 15, 2006.

Week Ten Commitment: On your next date, be sincere and communicate with your date. Spend time talking about things you each enjoy, and discover something fun you can do together on a future date. Then make a note of how you feel your communication went and how you can improve next time.

How My Dating Communication Went:

_____

_____

_____

_____

_____

_____

_____

_____

_____

_____

_____

_____

How I Will Improve on the Next Date:

_____

_____

_____

_____

_____

_____

_____

_____

_____

_____

_____

Part 4:

Stay Anxiously Engaged

11

Be Positive

Thanking, Thanking, and Thanking Some More

This earth is not our home. We are away at school, trying to master the lessons of "the great plan of happiness" so we can return home and know what it means to be there. Over and over the Lord tells us why the plan is worth our sacrifice—and His. Eve called it "the joy of our redemption" (Moses 5:11). Jacob called it "that happiness which is prepared for the saints" (2 Nephi 9:43). Of necessity, the plan is full of thorns and tears—His and ours. But because He and we are so totally in this together, our being "at one" with Him in overcoming all opposition will itself bring us "incomprehensible joy" (See Alma 28:8).
—Elder Bruce C. Hafen[1]

Have you ever noticed that people who are upbeat and positive tend to have the most friends? Having a positive mind-set opens doors, especially in dating. When we are genuinely happy and look for the goodness in people, people become interested in us and in our stories. Deep, enriching, and satisfying relationships can then be built.

Jimmy F. says, "You've just got to be positive no matter what. If things are disappointing, just realize that 'this too shall pass.' "

Jasmine C. says, "I try to see the good things about people. You get to know a person by trying to see their good qualities, seeing what makes them who they are."

Never Give Up

Now granted, each of us is probably destined to endure tough and challenging days. But the way we approach and deal with the set-backs and trials we face will ultimately determine our character and the contributions we will make to the world. In devastating situations, do we develop a self-pitying, "why me" attitude? Or do we focus our energies on being thankful for all of our precious blessings?

 Self-pity is easily the most destructive of the non-pharmaceutical narcotics; it is addictive, gives momentary pleasure and separates the victim from reality.—John W. Gardner

Whenever you are doing your best and you fail, you can celebrate. Seriously. In fact, the only way to succeed is to fail. The following is the background of a man who faced several challenges. See if you can determine who he was. Here are the facts about him:

- His family was forced out of their home. He had to work to support them.
- His mother died.
- He failed in business.
- He interviewed to get his dream job and failed.
- He then lost his job that he had.
- He wanted to go to college but couldn't qualify.
- He borrowed some money from a friend to start a business and by the end of the year was bankrupt. He spent the next seventeen years of his life paying off that debt.
- He was engaged to be married but his sweetheart died, and his heart was broken.
- He had a total nervous breakdown and was in bed for six months.
- He ran for political office three times in a row and lost.
- He married his new sweetheart.
- He ran for Congress and won.
- He ran for re-election in Congress and lost.
- He ran for the Senate of the United States and lost.
- He sought the Vice-Presidential nomination and got less than a hundred votes.
- He ran for the Senate again and lost.
- He was then elected President of the United States.

This persistent man was none other than Abraham Lincoln, one of the greatest leaders this world has ever seen. What characterized him? He never, ever gave up. He had a vision that he had been called to achieve something great, and he did not relent. He simply would not stop until his goals were fulfilled. Certainly those attributes served him as he led the nation in overcoming its greatest trial up to that time—the destructive Civil War. We can certainly follow this example. Our goal may not be to lead the United States as President, but we can achieve it, whatever it may be. You can be happily married in a relationship that President Gordon B. Hinckley suggested would be one that represents "the stuff of which your dreams are made."[2] Just never, ever give up.

 For every beauty there is an eye somewhere to see it. For every truth there is an ear somewhere to hear it. For every love there is a heart somewhere to receive it.—Ivan Panin

Some people may think that no one can understand what they have gone through. They may feel unheard, misunderstood, and alienated, especially as friends and family seem to only listen partially to their frustrations. And yet, the belief that no one else completely understands is simply not true. Jesus Christ can and does. He is your Savior and understands every one of your frustrations, setbacks, rejections, and losses. Abinadi testified that the Savior is no stranger to disappointment, discouragement, and pain:

> He is despised and rejected of men; a man of sorrows, and acquainted with grief; and we hid as it were our faces from him; he was despised, and we esteemed him not. Surely he has borne our griefs, and carried our sorrows; yet we did esteem him stricken, smitten of God, and afflicted. But he was wounded for our transgressions, he was bruised for our iniquities; the chastisement of our peace was upon him; and with his stripes we are healed. (Mosiah 14:3–5)

This fundamental principle—along with acknowledging that God is our Heavenly Father and we are His children whom He loves—brings great joy and personal power. By believing sincerely in your power to do God's will despite difficult circumstances, you become a powerful force on the earth.

James had recently returned home after serving a faithful mission. He went on a few dates before his mission, but was now ready to move forward in dating for a great marriage. During the course of the month of October, James asked fourteen different girls out, only to be rejected by every one of them. What did he do? Did he give up? Never. James persisted, focused on what he could control, remembering that the Savior would always be there for him. That is, he never gave up. In fact, he called that month his "0 for 14 October" month and kept asking girls out in November. Soon he went on some great dates with wonderful girls. He is now happily on his way to being married. The key was that James didn't let his disappointment destroy him.

Brother Curt Brinkman is a Boston Marathon world record holder, despite being in a wheelchair because of an accident wherein he lost his legs. He said the following in an interview. "Life is a great journey. Actually it's probably several races. There are obstacles everywhere, and it's our challenge to overcome them. Always get up when you fall down. As we hear so many times, the greatest problem with people is that when they fail, they fear to get back up again. Successful people are the ones who get back up over and over."[3]

Often, amidst the greatest challenges, it can feel like the whole world is against you or falling down around you. Not so coincidentally, this seems to happen after such traumatizing things as breakups.

Charles G. says, "My focus is to roll with the punches and be better not bitter."

Carol M. says, "When challenges come, and they will, get advice from your parents or your bishop or some friends. They'll help you keep your head on straight even when things are hard."

This path of persistence is certainly laden with more rocks, stones, and even booby traps than you can imagine. By taking the high road of full activity in the Lord's church and only settling for a temple marriage to a righteous eternal companion, you set yourself up for incredible challenges. Fortunately, the Lord is never one to leave you alone. As you live right and endure to the end, even the end of dating, the Lord will work through you to achieve amazing results. Sister Kristen Oaks said:

> It can be very painful to be single for such a long time, especially in a church of families. I know how it feels. On my 50th birthday my brother-in-law was reading the newspaper. He said,

"Hey, it says here in the paper that at age 50 your chances for getting killed by terrorists are better than your chances for getting married." I knew that dating was tough when he said that, but don't give up. It isn't a terrorist activity.

I would also say to you, be balanced. As a single woman, I had to go forward. I got a doctorate and became so involved in my profession that I forgot about being a good person. I would say to everyone in this room, always remember that your first calling is as a mother or as a father. Develop those domestic talents—talents of love and talents of service. As a single, I had to go searching for service projects, and now I have one every night across the table. I'm so thankful for that.[4]

Be Grateful

Columnist Jenkins Lloyd Jones put it this way:

Anyone who imagines that bliss is normal is going to waste a lot of time running around and shouting that he has been robbed. The fact of the matter is that most putts don't drop, most beef is tough, most children grow up to be just people, most successful marriages require a high degree of mutual toleration, most jobs are more often dull than otherwise. Life is like an old time rail journey . . . delays, sidetracks, smoke, dust, cinders and jolts, interspersed only occasionally by beautiful vistas and thrilling bursts of speed. The trick is to thank the Lord for letting you have the ride.[5]

One wise old woman whose husband had passed away said, "I spend half my time counting my blessings and the other half of my time thanking the Lord for them. So I have no time to complain." There are so many things to be grateful for in our lives. Some of those blessings are surely our family, friends, knowledge of the gospel, and the Atonement that Jesus Christ rendered for us, making it possible to one day achieve eternal life. Even going down to a more basic level, the food that we eat, the clothing we wear, and our homes and various places of shelter.

As we go about our daily lives, amazing things happen to us. We are the recipients of kind words and compliments from others. We have the opportunity to go to new places, have new experiences, and meet new people. Life is rich with opportunities waiting for us. Regarding not getting discouraged in dating, President Gordon B. Hinckley said, "Do not give up hope. And do not give up trying. But do give up being obsessed with it. The chances are that if you forget about it and become anxiously engaged in other activities, the prospects will brighten immeasurably."[6]

Anne G. says, "Be appreciative of all the things a guy does for you. Do nice things for him and mention how much you appreciate what he does."

When we pay compliments to others we are in essence showing them that we appreciate the efforts they are making. Sincere compliments not only strengthen the bond of friendship between you and your date, but they greatly increase the likelihood of your date having positive responses toward you in the future. Even if things don't work out with your date, at least you know you can value each other as individuals. This can definitely aid you in wanting to act civil toward them when you see them at church or other social gatherings. Also, by paying them sincere compliments during the time that the two of you are going on dates, it will make it a lot harder to gossip or say bad things about them to others.

Just as the power of compliments strengthens a dating relationship, the power of criticism quickly destroys a potential dating relationship. In one case we heard of, Taylor had asked Susan on a date. He thought she was attractive and noticed she was active in her ward. When Taylor took Susan to dinner, he tried to get positive conversation going. After asking some questions about Susan's hometown, family, and interests, Taylor was even more impressed with Susan. After dinner, they went to a play. On the way there, Susan made some sarcastic comments about Taylor regarding the way he looked and about his interests. Susan was clearly being critical of Taylor while Taylor had been nothing less than a gentleman on the date. His response? Taylor asked Susan why she made the comments that she did, and she told him to lighten up and that she was just kidding.

They watched the play and enjoyed it together. Then as they drove back to Susan's house, Susan made another negative comment about Taylor, this time regarding his "poor driving." At that point, Taylor told Susan he appreciated the fact that she had spent some time with him on the date, but emphasized that he was disappointed in her sarcastic, negative words. He told her that for that reason he would no longer ask her out. Susan was shocked, and she seriously thought that Taylor knew she was joking about every single comment. What she didn't know was that nobody besides her got the joke. In your dating, never degrade yourself by stooping to negativity, criticism, sarcasm, or ridicule. Those types of behaviors only demonstrate your lack of social awareness or self-monitoring, and those behaviors literally scream out to the world, "I can't handle respecting anyone! I'm unfit for marriage! I want to be old, gray, and alone for the rest of my existence!"

Each of us is a son or daughter of God with divine potential. When we see those whom we are dating as Heavenly Father views them, we will treat them with respect. In the end, if our interest level in them doesn't extend beyond friends or acquaintances we can at least walk away feeling no regrets for the way we treated them and glad that we were able to show sincere gratitude toward them for the efforts they made and the way they valued us.

Remain Realistic

> And see that all these things are done in wisdom and order; for it is not requisite that a man should run faster than he has strength. And again, it is expedient that he should be diligent, that thereby he might win the prize; therefore, all things must be done in order. —King Benjamin (Mosiah 3:27)

According to the world, falling in love is just a matter of randomly meeting that special someone, hearing the background music, and having fluffy feelings fill your heart. Romance, by Hollywood standards, is purely chemical. Romance, by the Lord's standards, is something much more elevated in nature. Yes, it includes "stuff that dreams are made of," but it also includes an open-eyed perspective of reality. In this sense, preparing for marriage is much like preparing for a mission or anything extremely difficult. In his article "Making Ourselves a Perfect Fit for Marriage," author Orson Scott Card said:

> Romance is nice. But it is biological in origin. That dizzy head-over-heels feeling is a species of losing your mind, and most of the time it lasts only as long as the chase. What we keep forgetting is that in marriage, as opposed to romances, you aren't marrying the thrilling wonderful perfect Someone you're looking at right now. You're marrying the man who decides not to have the dazzling career with the high salary, refusing promotions and transfers so the kids don't have to change schools. You're marrying the woman whose body

doesn't bounce back after the third baby, so she's no longer slim and attractive by the standards of the magazines. You're marrying the migraines and the hemorrhoids and the heart attack and the cancer; you're marrying the irritable, forgetful, lazy, thoughtless, sarcastic, distracted, too-busy days as well as the Kodak-happy ones.

You're marrying the one who works with you to raise the retarded or crippled child, or stands with you at the graveside of the child who dies. You're marrying the one who can't find work after the company folds or he's laid off; you're marrying the early Alzheimer's, the diabetes, the obesity, the pain of conflict and the struggle of forgiveness. The foundation of that isn't some ideal of romantic love. It's a commitment based on the goals you share. And real love, married love, is not what you start with—it's what you create together along the way. How foolish, when our young people wait to find love, or to have God show them their foreordained mate, instead of rationally looking at the eligible people and choosing someone who can and will live up to the commitment of marriage, someone with shared faith, someone with whom you can establish friendship and affection.[7]

Just as the mission of the Church is the "perfecting of the Saints," the mission of marriage is the perfecting of each other. And it certainly doesn't happen all at once. In this case, realistic expectations are a blessing.

Perfect, Perfect, Perfect

 Each heartfelt prayer, each Church meeting attended, each worthy friend, each righteous decision, each act of service performed all precede that goal of eternal life.
—President Thomas S. Monson[8]

There is freedom and power in exercising faith in the Atonement of Jesus Christ. But we are still imperfect beings, subject to imperfections and inadequacies. It is only in and through the Atonement that we tap into perfection and thus receive a remission of our sins. Why is this important in dating? By perfecting ourselves in Christ, we increase confidence before God and men. This empowers us to achieve success in any righteous endeavor we are pursuing. Moroni states it plainly:

Yea, come unto Christ, and be perfected in him, and deny yourselves of all ungodliness; and if ye shall deny yourselves of all ungodliness, and love God with all your might, mind, and strength, then is his grace sufficient for you, that by his grace ye may be perfect in Christ; and if by the grace of God ye are perfect in Christ, ye can in nowise deny the power of God. (Moroni 10:32)

Thus, the mission of the Church is the perfection of us. Yes, perfection. In other words, the injunction of Jesus Christ in the New Testament, repeated in the Book of Mormon, to "be ye therefore perfect" is attainable (3 Nephi 12:48, Matthew 5:48). But perfection does not mean one can be immediately sinless or totally competent in everything. Instead, it is to be whole, to be healed in Christ. It is to allow Christ to literally fill our souls with completion and totality. It is to resist evil and temptation, to avoid Satan. It is to put off the natural man in favor of the spiritual, "yielding to the enticings of the Holy Spirit," becoming a Saint through the Atonement of Christ the Lord, and becoming "as a child, submissive, meek, humble, patient, full of love, willing to submit to all things which the Lord seeth fit to inflict upon him, even as a child doth submit to his father" (Mosiah 3:19).

In this quest, there will certainly be setbacks. There will be disappointments and struggles. Stress is no stranger to the disciple. But there will also be peace. It is true that man was created and empowered to achieve godhood, but it is also true that man must *decide on his own* to do so and that he will never be pushed. Satan wanted all men forced into obedient submission, subjected to the will of the Father by total governmental rule and eliminate their accountability. But the design and will of the Father, and of His Holy Son, Jesus Christ, has ever been to free the soul to achieve greatness as a being that is interdependent. Like the Lord told the Prophet Joseph, if we are grateful, our trials will "give [us] experience, and shall be for [our] good" (D&C 122:7).

As you move forward with faith, know that the Lord stands by your side. Stay optimistic, even though you may feel hurt by others. It is likely that at some point during your mortal life, you have been wronged in some way. We live in a fallen world with imperfect people everywhere (including us). And especially in dating, you can experience frustration and hurt. The worst experience in your life may be when someone "breaks up" with you. It can feel like someone has died—or like you have died—the pain can be so bad. But take courage and know that the Lord understands your pain. And not only that, remember that you need to move forward. Moving forward means letting go of the wrongs. Like a hot air balloon that needs to drop hefty bags of weight to rise, you need to let go and forgive.

Bryant S. Hinckley, father of President Gordon B. Hinckley, quoting Charles Wagner wrote, "In the very depths of yourself dig a grave. Let it be like some forgotten spot to which no path leads; and there, in the eternal silence, bury the wrongs you have suffered. Your heart will feel as if a weight has fallen from it and a divine peace come to abide with you."[9]

....

1. Bruce C. Hafen, "The Atonement: All for All," *Ensign,* May 2004, 98.
2. Gordon B. Hinckley, "Living Worthy of the Girl You Will Someday Marry," *Ensign,* May 1998.
3. Curt Brinkman, interviewed by the authors.
4. Kristen Oaks, "Dating versus Hanging Out," *Ensign,* June 2006, 10-16.
5. Jenkins Lloyd Jones, "Big Rock Candy Mountains," *Deseret News,* June 12, 1973. Jenkins Lloyd Jones was a favorite columnist of President Gordon B. Hinckley. (See "God Shall Give unto You Knowledge by His Holy Spirit," BYU Devotional Address, Sept. 25, 1973.)
6. Gordon B. Hinckley, "Women of the Church," *Ensign*, Nov. 1996.
7. Orson Scott Card, "Making Ourselves a Perfect Fit in Marriage," In the Village, *Mormon Times,* April 24, 2008.
8. Thomas S. Monson, "Decisions Determine Destiny," CES Fireside, November 6, 2005. http://speeches.byu.edu/reader/reader. php?id=10726
9. Charles Wagner quoted by Bryant S. Hinckley, *That Ye Might Have Joy* (Salt Lake City: Bookcraft, 1958), 59.

WEEK ELEVEN COMMITMENT: Think of all the things you are most grateful for and focus on them this week. Tell your date about them, and listen to what he or she says.

The Top Ten Things I'm Most Grateful For:

1. _____

2. _____

3. _____

4. _____

5. _____

6. _____

7. _____

8. _____

9. _____

10. _____

12

Move Forward

Enduring to the End of Dating—and Beyond!

Two individuals approaching the marriage altar must realize that to attain the happy marriage which they hope for they must know that marriage . . . means sacrifice, sharing, and even a reduction of some personal liberties. It means long, hard economizing. It means children who bring with them financial burdens, service burdens, care and worry burdens; but also it means the deepest and sweetest emotions of all.
—President Spencer W. Kimball[1]

Sean R. says, "You need to be okay with being independent, but also recognize the obvious and immediate need for companionship in life. There is powerful synergy that can come from two people uniting together for a common purpose, to serve each other and serve Heavenly Father as a marriage unit."

Begin a New Chapter

But one of the attributes of love, like art, is to bring harmony and order out of chaos, to introduce meaning and affect where before there was none, to give rhythmic variations, highs and lows to a landscape that was previously flat.
—Molly Haskell

For every one of us who dates with the intent to marry, the truth is that we are learning to truly love an eternal companion for the first time. Though we existed for thousands of years in the presence of Heavenly

Father prior to this life, none of us were married. We simply made the decision to come to earth and become like Heavenly Father through the process of faith, repentance, baptism, being confirmed a member of the Church of Jesus Christ of Latter-day Saints, and receiving the gift of the Holy Ghost to help us on our way. This leaves much of dating and marriage a mystery to be explored. And yet, you cannot risk having a false perspective on what dating and marriage truly are. Writer Jenkins Lloyd Jones said:

> There seems to be a superstition among many thousands of our young who hold hands and smooch in the drive-ins that marriage is a cottage surrounded by perpetual hollyhocks to which a perpetually young and handsome husband comes home to a perpetually young and ravishing wife. When the hollyhocks wither and boredom and bills appear the divorce courts are jammed. . . . Anyone who imagines that bliss is normal is going to waste a lot of time running around shouting that he has been robbed.[2]

Hollywood teaches that you can have pure pleasure from dating and marriage without any of the responsibility. No wonder so many actors and actresses are on their third and fourth marriages, still wandering the world in search of that "pure pleasure without a price" situation. What does that mean for the rest of us? We can learn from other people's experiences what makes marriages work, and what doesn't. You'll probably find most of your assumptions confirmed, but you may be surprised. Look closely at the great marriages and you'll discover why they are what they are.

Chris shares:

> I interviewed a woman who had been happily married to her husband for several decades. Together, they had fourteen children (all theirs), who so far had all served missions and married in the temple. At first, I thought that her answers to all my questions would be Pollyanish, or at least a little naïve. I believed, for some reason, that she might have just been born a "Super Mom," destined to achieve her purpose. Although it was true that her parents had raised her well, this woman had clearly worked hard to become Christlike. One of the things that her husband let me know later was that through all those years of marriage, she had never once criticized him. Yes, she had disagreed often, and they had discussed those disagreements. But she had never criticized him. That kind of love was clearly part of the reason for their success in marriage.

So often singles think that true love involves finding that one right person in the world that you can spend eternity with. They may know and even state that they don't believe in a "one and only," but they often turn around and date as if they're only looking for that one person that will sweep them off their feet immediately. In this world of fast food, fast Internet, and fast cars, is it any surprise that this desire for fast exaltation exists? One stake president described the reality of the dating challenge when he said, "People aren't born soul mates. Through proper dating, courtship, and marriage, you become soul mates." In other words, with the help of the Lord and the other person, you create it all—every hope, every dream, every feeling, every wonderful experience together, every longing, and every joy.

Allan S. says, "You should be able to come at dating and marriage from two different angles and accomplish more powerful results than you could alone. That's where the power of marriage is, where you have two people coming together to become one, and it is more powerful than either could have achieved separately."

Surely this path of total commitment to the Lord and your spouse is one of great effort and patience. As you move forward and become more serious about a certain dating prospect, you come closer to realizing the fulfillment of the Lord's promises. This path is not cheap or easy, and it doesn't end with engagement or marriage. If marriage is your only goal, you will likely be disappointed after the honeymoon. That is, marriage, just like other life experiences—like going to college or serving a full-time mission—is a new beginning. Marriage is a new opportunity to serve, learn, and grow in love for the Savior, and love for your spouse. And millions testify that in marriage, you can find the greatest joy you have ever experienced. But that is often after months and years of challenging and (yes) wonderful and awfully challenging work.

 Life is not easy for any of us. But what of that? We must have perseverance and above all confidence in ourselves. We must believe that we are gifted for something and that this thing must be attained.—Marie Curie

In Victor Frankl's seminal book *Man's Search for Meaning*, he maintains that a powerful sense of purpose will overcome any bad circumstances. While he was being tortured in the Nazi death camps,

Frankl found strength in envisioning the image of his wife and conversing with her. Frankl said:

> We stumbled on in the darkness, over big stones and through large puddles, along the one road leading from the camp. The accompanying guards kept shouting at us and driving us with the butts of their rifles. . . . Occasionally I looked at the sky, where the stars were fading and the pink light of the morning was beginning to spread behind a dark bank of clouds. But my mind clung to my wife's image, imagining it with an uncanny acuteness. I heard her answering me, saw her smile, her frank and encouraging look. Real or not, her look was then more luminous than the sun which was beginning to rise.
>
> A thought transfixed me: for the first time in my life I saw the truth as it is set into song by so many poets, proclaimed as the final wisdom by so many thinkers. The truth—that love is the ultimate and the highest goal to which man can aspire.[3]

During the struggles in life, envision yourself with your righteous spouse, whom you love (and may not even know yet). Do it often, even when it seems absurd. It will help you to create a reservoir of strength and power to face daily difficulties. Many happily married individuals report that positively envisioning their spouse helped them greatly. This holds true, especially in the cases of those who married in advanced years.

 Love seems the swiftest, but it is the slowest of all growths. No man or woman really knows what perfect love is until they have been married a quarter of a century.—Mark Twain

Prepare yourself for the adventure of marriage by dating right. As you become more serious about the person you are dating, be careful not to rush things too quickly. Most marriage experts recommend dating someone for at least a full year before considering marriage. This is good general advice, but be sensitive to the Spirit. If the Spirit prompts you to marry in twelve months, then do it. If it prompts you to wait and marry in two years, then do it. If it prompts you to move forward and marry in six months, then do it. Everyone is different, and the Lord knows exactly what His children need.

President Hinckley stated, "I hope you will not put off marriage too long. I do not speak so much to the young women as to the young men whose prerogative and responsibility it is to take the lead in this matter. Don't go on endlessly in a frivolous dating game. Look for a choice companion, one you can love, honor, and respect, and make a decision."[5]

Regardless of their level of personal confidence, some singles that have been in the dating game for an extended period of time get the idea that they are not "marriage material." Nothing could be further from the truth. Nephi said, in his classic declaration in 1 Nephi 3:7, "I know that the Lord giveth no commandments unto the children of men, save he shall prepare a way for them that they may accomplish the thing which he commandeth them" (emphasis added). In other words, the commandment to marry is in full force for everyone, so everyone who obeys the Lord is marriage material. The fact is, everyone should be anxiously engaged and working toward an eternal marriage, and the Lord will take care of the rest. After all, most people do not have the goal of being a ministering angel for eternity. Go for the gold, and you will eventually get it.

Keep the Lord First

Throughout the dating process, temptations constantly come in the form of pride, lust, envy, and so many other negative emotions. The most dangerous of all is that of putting something, or even *someone*, above the Lord. When put to the test, you must always place the Lord first in your life. It can be a temptation, especially in dating, to think more of and put more emphasis on the person you are interested than anyone else, even the Lord. This is a mistake, and it can prove devastating. There once was a young man who was very interested in marrying a young woman he was dating. He had dated her for several months and felt good about asking her to marry him. Then, desiring greater confirmation of his decision, he asked Heavenly Father if it was right. He immediately had a stupor of thought and felt uncomfortable with the idea of marrying her. He literally felt that the Lord had told him not to marry her. But the young man really liked her.

Despite the Lord's warnings, the young man moved forward and he married the young woman in the temple. Several years later, his wife stopped attending church and left him for another man, abandoning him and their three children. At first, he was plagued with what had happened. How could this have happened to him of all people? Hadn't he prayed about his decision? Then, he remembered the Lord's decisive answer to him that he should not marry her. In the end, shame and guilt remained as this man shamefully learned the consequences of his disobedience to the voice of the Lord.

Listen to the Lord, especially in terms of dating and marriage where the consequences are absolutely eternal. Granted, marriages can fail for a variety of reasons. But when the Lord tells you something about someone you are dating, it is not a time to question, but simply to obey. How do you put the Lord first in dating? First of all, ensure that you "pray always" (D&C 10:5) and "counsel with the Lord in all thy doings" (Alma 37:37). As you do, the answers and guidance will be there in the Lord's timing. President Thomas S. Monson explained it powerfully in this way:

> Though the task seems large, we are strengthened by the truth: "The greatest force in this world today is the power of God as it works through man." If we are on the Lord's errand, we are entitled to the Lord's help. That divine help, however, is predicated upon our worthiness. To sail safely the seas of mortality, to perform a human rescue mission, we need the guidance of that eternal mariner—even the great Jehovah. We look up, we reach out to obtain heavenly help.[6]

Jake D. said, "Always involve the Lord in your dating."

Get Anxiously and Carefully Engaged

 A lady's imagination is very rapid; it jumps from admiration to love, from love to matrimony, in a moment.
—Jane Austen, *Pride and Prejudice*

How will the Lord answer your prayer about whom to marry? Remember that you are responsible for you, and you can pray to know your path. But, it is not your responsibility to pray to know the path of someone else who is not in your stewardship. In other words, if a young man asks God if he should marry a young woman, God can tell him it is right, but the young man cannot impose that answer on the young woman. She has to receive her own revelation.

In cases of courtship, the Lord has clearly stated his case for prayer:

But, behold, I say unto you, that you must study it out in your mind; then you must ask me if it be right, and if it is right I will cause that your bosom shall burn within you; therefore, you shall feel that it is right.

But if it be not right you shall have no such feelings, but you shall have a stupor of thought that shall cause you to forget the thing which is wrong; therefore, you cannot write that which is sacred save it be given you from me. (Doctrine and Covenants 9:8–9)

If our love is only a will to possess, it is not love.
—Thich Nhat Hanh

Sometimes daters, especially some men, tend to think that because they have strong feelings for another person, that person should automatically share those same feelings. When you begin dating someone seriously and are interested in an eternal relationship with him or her, never forget that that person has agency. And ultimately, he or she may not actually feel the same way you do about the relationship. If you want to be with that person for eternity, it is your job then to present your case as best you can by showing love, and then letting him or her make a decision. And be willing to let go, if necessary.

One may embrace the principle of agency, but still be totally frustrated with it. Oftentimes in dating, however, the fact that one is willing to let the other person "stretch their wings and fly" is the very key that makes the relationship successful.

Choose in the Right Way

As confidence in a relationship increases, some single men make the mistake of projecting their own level of interest on the chosen young woman. This presents a problem, especially if the young woman has no real interest in the guy. This can lead to major disappointment and frustration. But can such things be avoided? Yes, if a single man focuses on keeping things in perspective and understanding that he can only receive revelation for himself.

In life, we often expect things to be easy. Marriage is certainly not one of those things. Spend a few minutes talking with any happily married couple, and it will quickly become obvious that a great courtship and marriage takes an incredible amount of daily effort. There are no shortcuts. One of the keys to success is to think spiritually rather than naturally.

Overcome Setbacks

 By perseverance the snail reached the ark.
—Charles Haddon Spurgeon

Wisdom, knowledge, and great spiritual blessings like marriage require a price. They take time and our best efforts and prayers. As you seek for comfort and strength in your amazing journey, there are many scriptures that can provide you with power to overcome challenges.

Chris says:

> When I was dating Julia, I quickly realized she was the one I wanted to marry. She was beautiful, focused, educated, and full of testimony. I didn't tell her early on that I wanted to marry her, of course, but I stayed focused and did everything I could to demonstrate my love for her. But there were definitely challenges that presented themselves. I started wondering how I could be a great husband, and how I could provide for my wife and new family that would later come. But I prayed for faith, and the Lord granted it to me.
>
> On one occasion, after I started dating Julia, I was driving her car by myself back from the store when the car was suddenly rear ended. The vehicle spun in circles and rolled. As it hurled through the air, I felt my body experiencing the full force of gravity, and I feared the worst. To me, it was almost as though time stopped for a moment. And, in my heart I prayed that I might marry Julia before I died. As the car crashed down, the windows split and glass shattered everywhere. I was blessed to walk out of that car with only a scratch on my arm. Truly the Lord protected me. And when I joyfully looked at Julia across the altar in the temple, I knew the Lord had fulfilled every promise He had made.

 Explore your higher latitudes. . . . Be a Columbus to whole new continents and worlds within you, open new channels, not of trade but of thought.—Henry David Thoreau

The path toward godhood is one that includes real challenges. But it also includes great joy and indescribable happiness. Regarding dating for marriage, one wise man said, "It is what you make it. Make it awful or make it great. And that's what it will be." We, the authors, challenge you to do the latter—make it great. And know that Heavenly Father will always be there to assist you.

In reference to the incredible new opportunities in life, the old adage goes, "the best is yet to come!" And for you, it definitely is. . . .

• •

1. Spencer W. Kimball, *Teachings of the Presidents of the Church: Spencer W. Kimball* (Salt Lake City: The Church of Jesus Christ of Latter-day Saints, 2006), 194.
2. Jenkins Lloyd Jones, "Big Rock Candy Mountains," *Deseret News*, June 12, 1973.
3. Victor Frankl, *Man's Search for Meaning* (Boston: Beacon Press, 2006), 56–7.
4. Gordon B. Hinckley, "Thou Shalt Not Covet," *Ensign,* Mar. 1990, 6.
5. Thomas S. Monson, "The Call for Courage," *Ensign,* May 2004, 57.

WEEK TWELVE COMMITMENT: Take whatever steps you need to right now to be better prepared for a serious dating relationship and a happy eternal marriage.

Thoughts, Goals, and Promptings

_____
_____
_____
_____
_____
_____
_____
_____
_____
_____
_____
_____
_____
_____
_____
_____
_____
_____
_____
_____
_____
_____
_____
_____
_____
_____

About the Authors

Chris Deaver has taught youth and young adults at seminaries, EFY, institutes, and firesides throughout the country. He has been published in the *New Era* and *Friend* magazines. Chris works as a professional consultant at Dell and co-founded a 501(c)3 non-profit: the International Mentoring Network Organization dedicated to mentoring. Prior to that, he served a mission to Peru and then taught in the Missionary Training Center for several years. He also authored the book *Know Before You Go*. Chris earned a BA in animation, and an MBA from Brigham Young University. He is a triathlete, and enjoys studying the martial arts and drawing ridiculous cartoons. He loves spending time with his wife, Julia, and sons Daniel and Austin.

Julia Deaver dedicates her time to being a mom to her two wonderful sons, Danny and Austin. She enjoys asthetics, cooking, shopping for a deal, and serving in the Church. Since completing a full-time mission to the Dominican Republic, she has been involved in the Young Women organization and teaching youth in Sunday School and at firesides. She authors an ongoing magazine column titled "Beauty on a Budget." Julia studied marriage, family, and human development at Ricks College and BYU, and graduated from Bon Losee as a Master Esthetician. She now works from home with Exfuze, a multi-botanical extract supplement company and does very well. In addition, Julia has given humanitarian service in various places, including four months in an orphanage in Ecuador.

Don McCartney served a full-time mission to Munich, Germany, graduated from BYU with a BS in finance, and has worked for several years in the pharmaceutical industry. He has adventured through many cities and states throughout his life including San Jose, Boston, and Washington, DC, and knocked doors throughout the greater Provo, Utah, area to interact with and interview young adult singles. He has been featured in publications including *The Daily Universe*. Don has served in the Church as a Sunday School president, in elders quorum presidencies, and a ward activities committee member. He has excelled in several competitive sports including Church basketball and broom hockey.

0 26575 53412 2